Building a
Data Warehouse
for Decision Support

Vidette Poe

with contributions by Laura L. Reeves

For book and bookstore information

http://www.prenhall.com
gopher to gopher.prenhall.com

Prentice Hall PTR
Upper Saddle River, NJ 07458

Library of Congress Cataloging-In-Publication Data

Poe, Vidette.
　　Building a data warehouse for decision support / Vidette Poe;
with contributions by Laura Reeves.
　　　p.　cm.
　　Includes index.
　　ISBN 0–13–371121–8
　　1. Decision support systems.　2. Database design.　I. Title
T58.62.P63　1995
658.4′038—dc20　　　　　　　　　　　　　　　95–25096
　　　　　　　　　　　　　　　　　　　　　　　　　CIP

Acquisitions editor: Mark Taub
Cover designer: Design Source
Cover director: Jerry Votta
Manufacturing buyer: Alexis R. Heydt
Compositor/Production services: Pine Tree Composition, Inc.

© 1996 by Prentice Hall PTR
Prentice-Hall, Inc.
A Simon & Schuster Company
Upper Saddle River, New Jersey 07458

The publisher offers discounts on this book when ordered in
bulk quantities.

For more information contact:
　　Corporate Sales Department
　　Prentice Hall PTR
　　One Lake Street
　　Upper Saddle River, New Jersey 07458

　　Phone: 800-382-3419
　　FAX: 201-236-7141
　　email: corpsales@prenhall.com

Printed in the United States of America
10　9　8　7　6　5　4　3　2　1

ISBN: 0-13-371121-8

Prentice Hall International (UK) Limited, *London*
Prentice Hall of Australia Pty. Limited, *Sydney*
Prentice Hall Canada, Inc., *Toronto*
Prentice Hall Hispanoamericana, S.A., *Mexico*
Prentice Hall of India Private Limited, *New Delhi*
Prentice Hall of Japan, Inc., *Tokyo*
Simon & Schuster Asia Pte. Ltd., *Singapore*
Editora Prentice Hall do Brasil, Ltda., *Rio de Janeiro*

To the Love of my Life
With thanks.

Contents

Preface   *xv*

Acknowledgements   *xxiii*

Chapter 1   *Let's Start with the Basics*   **1**

WHAT IS A DECISION SUPPORT SYSTEM?   3
UNDERSTANDING OPERATIONAL VERSUS
   ANALYTICAL PROCESSING   3
WHAT IS A DATA WAREHOUSE?   6
REAL LIFE DATA WAREHOUSE EXAMPLES   6
  Community Mutual Insurance Company   7
    A Corporate Overview   7
    Meeting the Need for Information—Predecessor Systems   7
    In the Beginning . . .   8
    Gathering Data Requirements   8
    Infrastructures   9
    User Reaction to Initial Development   9
    The User Community   10
    Building on the Warehouse   11
    What the Future Holds   11
    20/20 Hindsight   12
     Tips from the Trenches 1.1:   LEARNING FROM COMMUNITY
     MUTUAL INTERNAL COST ALLOCATIONS: CHARGEBACKS   13
  A Consumer Packaged Goods Company   14
    A Corporate Overview   14
    How it Got Started   14
    Implementation Project   14
    Architecture and Infrastructure   15
    End User Reaction   16
    Data Warehouse Expansion   17
    20/20 Hindsight   17
SUMMARY   18
ENDNOTE   18

Chapter 2 *Understanding Terms and Technology* **21**

ANALYTICAL PROCESSING 23
OPERATIONAL PROCESSING 23
DECISION SUPPORT SYSTEMS 23
DATA WAREHOUSE 24
ENVIRONMENT FOR DATA ACCESS 24
ARCHITECTURE 24
TECHNICAL INFRASTRUCTURES 26
SOURCE AND TARGET DATA 28
LEVELS OF USERS 28
CLASSES OF TOOLS 29
DECISION SUPPORT SYSTEM (DSS) APPLICATIONS 30
DATA TRANSFORMATION 30
DATA TRANSFORMATION TOOLS 31
MIDDLEWARE TOOLS 31
METADATA 31
STAR SCHEMA 33
HIERARCHIES 33
GRANULARITY 33
DATABASE GATEWAY 34
MEGABYTES, GIGABYTES, AND TERABYTES 34
DECISION SUPPORT DEVELOPMENT CYCLE 34
SUMMARY 35

Chapter 3 *Understanding Architecture and Infrastructures* **37**

THE TASK AT HAND 39
UNDERSTANDING DATA WAREHOUSE ARCHITECTURE 40
THE CHARACTERISTICS OF DATA WAREHOUSE
   ARCHITECTURE 40
   Data Is Extracted from Source Systems, Database, or Files 41

The Data from the Source Systems is Integrated
and Transformed before Being Loaded
into the Data Warehouse   42

A Separate Read-only Database is Created for Decision
Support Data   44

Users Access the Data Warehouse via a Front End Tool
or Application   44

EXPANDING THE GENERIC DATA WAREHOUSE
ARCHITECTURE   45

UNDERSTANDING THE RELATIONSHIP
OF INFRASTRUCTURES AND ARCHITECTURE   50

ARCHITECTURE AND INFRASTRUCTURES
AS A SEPARATE PROJECT   56

　　Tips From the Trenches 3.1:
　　ARCHITECTURE AND INFRASTRUCTURES   57

AND THE ANSWER IS . . .   57

SUMMARY   59

Chapter 4　　*The Decision Support Life Cycle*　　**61**

LIFE CYCLES FOR SYSTEM DEVELOPMENT   63

ISSUES AFFECTING THE DECISION SUPPORT LIFE CYCLE   63

THE DECISION SUPPORT LIFE CYCLE
IN AN ARCHITECTED ENVIRONMENT   64

THE PHASES OF THE DECISION SUPPORT
LIFE CYCLE (DSLC)   65

Phase 1: Planning   65

Phase 2: Gathering Data Requirements
and Modeling   67

　Gathering Data Requirements   67

　Data Modeling   68

Phase 3: Physical Database Design
and Development   69

Phase 4: Data Mapping and Transformation   71

Phase 5: Populating the Data Warehouse   72

Tips from the Trenches 4.1:   AVAILABILIY OF DATA   73

Phase 6: Automating Data Management Procedures   74

Phase 7: Application Development—Creating
the Starter Set of Reports   75

Phase 8: Data Validation and Testing   76

Phase 9: Training   77

Phase 10: Rollout   77

SUMMARY   78

Chapter 5   *Getting Started with Data Warehouse Development*   *81*

THE PROOF IS IN THE PILOT   83

Clarify the Purpose and Goal of the Pilot Project   83

Treat the Pilot like a Development Project   85

Building on the Pilot   85

CHOOSING A BUSINESS AREA FOR DATA
WAREHOUSE DEVELOPMENT   87

Tips from the Trenches 5.1:   CHOOSING
A BUSINESS AREA   89

ENSURING A SUCCESSFUL DATA WAREHOUSE   89

Tips from the Trenches 5.2:   BUILDING
A SUCCESSFUL DATA WAREHOUSE "THE BIG EIGHT"   90

Be Clear on Your Goal   90

Understand the Chosen Data Warehouse Architecture   91

Make Sure the Technical Infrastructures Are in Place
or Being Put in Place   91

Clarify the Project Team's Responsibility
and Final Deliverable   91

Make Sure the Members of the Project Team Understand
the Difference between Operational and Decision
Support Data   92

Get the Correct Training   93

Get the Right Resources   93

Choose Front End Data Access Software Based
on User Needs and Abilities   95
SUMMARY   96

Chapter 6   Gathering Data Requirements   **99**

A PROPER MINDSET   101
USER INTERVIEWS   101
The Purpose of Interviews   101
Setting up Successful Interviews   102
Who to Interview   102
Tips from the Trenches 6.1:   SETTING UP SUCCESSFUL
INTERVIEWS   103
Key End Users and Analysts from the Target
Business Functions   104
Managers from the Target Business Functions   104
Analysts & Users from Related Business Functions   104
Managers from Related Business Functions   105
Executives   105
What to Ask End Users   105
Job Responsibilities   105
Current Analysis   106
Ad Hoc Analysis   106
Business Analyses   107
Data Specific Information   107
A Wish List   108
What to Ask Executives   109
Documenting What You Heard   110
What You Have to Know for DSS   111
DEVELOPING THE DATA MODEL   112
Dimensional Business Model   112
Logical Data Model   114

Tips from the Trenches 6.2: THE BASICS
OF DATA MODELING 115

SUMMARY 115

Chapter 7 *Designing the Database for a Data Warehouse* **117**

TRANSACTION-PROCESSING DATABASES 119

DECISION SUPPORT DATABASES 120

STAR SCHEMA DATABASE DESIGN 120

The Benefits of Using a Star Schema 121

Understanding Star Schema Design—Facts and Dimensions 121

VARIETIES OF STAR SCHEMAS 122

How to Read the Diagrams 122

Tips from the Trenches 7.1: UNDERSTANDING FACTS
AND DIMENSIONS 123

Simple Star Schemas 124

Multiple Fact Tables 125

Outboard Tables 127

Variations of a Star Schema 127

Multi-Star Schemas 129

A SALAD DRESSING EXAMPLE 131

Understanding the Available Data, Browsing
the Dimension Tables 133

Using Table Attributes 134

Creating Attribute Hierarchies 134

AGGREGATION 136

DENORMALIZAITON 137

DATA WAREHOUSE DATABASE DESIGN EXAMPLES 139

Reservation Database 139

Investment Database 139

Health Insurance Database 142

Putting It All Together 142

SUMMARY 142

Chapter 8   *Successful Data Access*   147

GENERAL UNDERSTANDING OF DATA ACCESS   149
WHAT ARE YOU REALLY TRYING TO DO?   149
TYPES OF ACCESS   150
LEVELS OF USERS   151
WHAT IS A DSS APPLICATION?   154
DATA ACCESS CHARACTERISTICS   155
   Visualization of the Data Warehouse   156
   User Formulates Request   156
      Metrics and Calculated Metrics   157
      Constraining a Request   158
   How the Request is Processed   159
   Presentation of Results   162
      Reports   162
      Graphs   162
      Maps   163
   Communicate Findings   163
   Advanced Features   163
      Advanced Analytics   163
      Batch Query Processing   164
   DSS Application Development   164
CLASSES OF TOOLS   165
   Data Access/Query Tools   165
   Report Writers   166
   Multidimensional Database Management Systems (MDBMS)   166
   Advanced DSS Tools   167
   Executive Information Systems (EIS)   167
   Tiered Architectures   168
DATA DESIGN REQUIREMENTS   169
METADATA   169
   Operational Metadata versus DSS Metadata 169
   Warehouse Changes   170

How Is DSS Metadata Used?   171
Application Deployment   171
SELECTING TOOLS FOR YOUR ORGANIZATION   172
One Tool Fits All?   172
The Request for Proposal (RFP)   172
Key Considerations   173
What Matters to You?   174
Selecting a Vendor Not Just a Tool   174
SUMMARY   175

Chapter 9   Training, Support, and Rollout   177

SUCCESS CRITERIA   179
TRAINING   179
SUPPORT   181
INTERNAL MARKETING OF THE DATA WAREHOUSE   182
DATA WAREHOUSE MARKETING IDEAS   182
Target Specific Groups   182
Get Clear and Visible Management Support   183
Provide Visible Opportunities   183
Be Proactive   184
Create a Publication   184
PLANNING A ROLLOUT: DEPLOYMENT   184
Phased Rollout Approach   184
Logistics of a Rollout   185
SUMMARY   185

Appendix   187

Index   205

Preface

Many corporations are actively looking for new technologies that will assist them in becoming more profitable and competitive. Gaining competitive advantage requires that companies accelerate their decision making process so that they can respond quickly to change. One key to this accelerated decision making is having the right information, at the right time, easily accessible.

Currently, data exists within the corporate business systems that can provide this decision making information. However, in most companies, this data is spread across multiple systems, platforms, and locations creating issues of data integrity and making access in a timely fashion next to impossible.

A data warehouse for decision support developed within an architected environment is designed specifically to supply this critical information to decision makers.

Advances in technology now make the development of a data warehouse providing credible and timely decision support information feasible. These technologies include:

- Open client server architectures
- Advanced techniques to replicate, refresh, and update data
- Tools to extract, transform, and load data from multiple, heterogeneous sources
- Databases specifically designed to handle very high volumes of data
- Front end data access and analysis software with extensive functionality

This book is about building a data warehouse for decision support in an architected environment. It is being written to provide practical and realistic guidelines for your data warehouse development project so that you can move forward in a knowledgeable and informed manner. It will clarify the aspects of development that are critical to success and those that are not. "Tips from the Trenches" will furnish practical tips, ideas, and ways to approach development that have been learned over the course of several data warehouse projects.

This book will provide a good understanding of the technical issues involved in building a data warehouse for decision support including:

- The life cycle for building decision support systems
- Data warehouse architectures
- Planning the data warehouse
- Gathering requirements from users and transforming them into a database schema
- Database design for a data warehouse
- The data access environment—successfully using the data warehouse

INTENDED AUDIENCE

The primary focus of this book is on the actual development of a data warehouse. The intended audience are the members of a project team whose task is to make the data warehouse work. This includes a broad range of data processing and business professionals including:

- Project Managers
- Data modelers and database designers
- DBAs
- Programmers and analysts
- System and data architects
- Users

This book presumes some understanding or experience with building systems in general, and a knowledge of relational database technology for the technical discussions.

Some aspects of this book may be too technical for users. However, it will provide them with a strong understanding of what a data warehouse is, how it is developed, the kinks in the development cycle, and why it may take a little longer than was first imagined. I would encourage users to read it.

HOW THIS BOOK IS STRUCTURED

This book was written to be both comprehensive and easy to understand. In an effort to convey as much as possible about data warehouse development, the chapters are structured to move through the data warehouse development life cycle as closely as possible to actual development.

Chapter 1 provides information on analytical databases and outlines their characteristics. It also provides two real life examples of data warehouses that are actively being used for decision support within the corporation. These two data warehouses have been chosen as examples because they are considered successful within the corporation and are actively being used by the user community. Although developed using entirely different approaches, both data warehouses have evolved over several years of development, which provides a realistic perspective on how these systems are built, what makes them successful, and allows for 20/20 hindsight which can be extremely helpful to companies just beginning development. The whole development team, users associated with the project, and anybody interested in a general understanding of the concepts of a data warehouse will find this chapter interesting.

Chapter 2 provides an overview of data warehouse terms and technology. Not just definitions, this chapter provides fundamental underlying concepts which will be used throughout the book.

Chapter 3 begins the process of defining data warehouse architectures and infrastructures—the "blueprint" of your data warehouse design and development. Architecture and infrastructures are some of the most important aspects of building a data warehouse, and this chapter is one of the most important in the book. Everyone on the project team should be required to read this chapter—as well as anyone with a general interest in how data warehouses are implemented.

Realizing that most people do not know how to put a project plan together for building a data warehouse, Chapter 4 was created. *The Decision Support Life Cycle* explains the phases of the life cycle of building a data warehouse and the primary focus of each phase. Although not down to the task level, this chapter is a comprehensive overview of what you need to pay attention to in developing a data warehouse for decision support.

Getting Started, Chapter 5, discusses different types of pilots, tips for a successful pilot project, choosing business areas, and the "Big 8"—critical issues will help ensure a successful development project.

Chapter 6—*Gathering Data Requirements* begins the focus on data and provides information on what data is needed, who to interview, and what kinds of questions to ask. We also discuss logical data models and introduce the concept of a Dimensional Business Model as a means of documenting what you learn in diagrammatic format.

In writing this book, choices about the best approach to database design for large, analytical databases had to be made. Hence, Chapter 7 was born, which delves into designing the data warehouse database, and is a primer on star schema database design. All data analysts, data modelers, DBAs (especially DBAs), and whoever is doing the actual database design should read and understand this chapter. Now when someone throws this strange term around, you'll not only know what it is, you'll know how to do it!

Chapter 8 is an extremely sophisticated chapter on data access and making accessible decision support information a reality within your corporation. This chapter will explain different classifications of tools, different levels of user, provide information to assist you in choosing tools for your information needs, and discuss DSS applications. Metadata is also covered in this chapter.

The final chapter is a short chapter on rolling out your

data warehouse—with some ideas on training, support, and in-house marketing that we thought were important.

This book covers the fundamental development issues you will need to address to build your data warehouse. Because of time constraints, other important issues, for instance, data replication technologies and the technicalities surrounding the scheduled update to the warehouse, have not been discussed in depth. Perhaps as more data warehouses are developed, you will find informative articles on these subjects that will assist you.

A well architected and designed data warehouse can, in fact, furnish your company with the decision support information it needs in a competitive market. Finding solutions to the technical issues surrounding the data warehouse, its integration into current system architectures, and successfully making all of the necessary components—the data transformation tools, the heterogeneous platforms and databases, the communications, networking and data replication technologies—work together makes these systems interesting and challenging to develop. This book will provide information to assist you with this challenge.

Acknowledgements

I would like to acknowledge assistance from many people in the development of this book.

My reviewers, Peggy Koop, James O'Reilly, and Kimberly Poe made valuable contributions to this manuscript and helped me stay focused on the fact that technical subjects can be taught with simplicity. I would like to acknowledge their valuable contributions to this book.

Laura Reeves has been designing decision support systems for many years and has a wide range of decision support knowledge and expertise. Currently with MicroStrategies, Inc., Laura was responsible for writing a comprehensive and sophisticated chapter on front end data access for the data warehouse. She also made technical and editorial contributions throughout this book. I am grateful for all of her assistance.

As writing timelines got tight, Red Brick Systems Inc. came through by graciously providing manuals and documentation so I didn't have to design a whole database from scratch to teach about star schema database design. I am extremely grateful for their contribution.

I would like to thank Linda Bronstein and Anne Meyers of Community Mutual for their time and energy in providing extensive information on the design and development of their data warehouse, which we used as an example in Chapter 1. They were knowledgeable about the technical aspects of a data warehouse, considerate, and wonderful to work with.

A special kind of thanks to the three little guys at home— you keep me smiling. You're right, it's time to go out and play.

Finally, to the women who have worked and studied with me for many years, and are changing the face of business and the technical arts, I salute you with this book.

Chapter 1

Let's Start with the Basics

WHAT IS A DECISION SUPPORT SYSTEM?

A decision support system is a system that provides information to users so that they can analyze a situation and make decisions. Put another way, a decision support system provides information to assist employees in making decisions and more effectively doing their jobs. This decision making can be long-term strategic decision making, such as analyzing buying patterns over several years to develop a new product or service or perhaps to introduce a product into a new European or Far Eastern location. Decision making could also be short term and tactical in nature, such as reviewing and changing recommended order quantities for a particular product. The systems providing this information so that employees are better equipped to make more informed decisions are decision support systems.

UNDERSTANDING OPERATIONAL VERSUS ANALYTICAL PROCESSING

When you hear people talking about the operational processing, they are referring to the systems that run the day-to-day business of a company. These often will be on-line transaction systems, which are updated continually throughout the day. For instance, if someone buys a printer from your computer store, the operational system will subtract one from the number of printers on hand at your site. As printers continue to sell throughout the day, the operational systems will consistently subtract (or make additions to in the case of shipment receipts) from the inventory. When the inventory reaches a specific level, these operational systems may automatically generate a purchase order for more stock from the supplier. This is an example of operational processing which handles the day to day operations of the business.

Analytical systems are systems that provide information used for analyzing a problem or situation. Analytical processing is primarily done through comparisons, or by analyzing patterns and trends. For instance, an analytical system might show you how a specific brand of printer is selling throughout different parts of the United States, and also how that specific brand is selling since it was first introduced into your stores. Comparing sales between the different territories within the United States can provide a certain type of analytical information, while scanning historical information will show you how the product is selling over time.

Analytical databases do not hold up-to-the-minute information, but hold information *as of a specific point in time*.[1] This makes perfect sense for a system that is providing information being used for comparisons and trending. Comparisons require a stable number *to compare to*. For instance, it is possible to ascertain that June's sales of printers were substantially lower than the previous three months because monthly sales figures are available for comparison. Sales figures for printers *as of month end* were stored in the database. It's possible to monitor printer sales *as of* the preceding day, the preceding week, the preceding month or year (or other period), if that is the level of information being held in the analytical database.

Trying to find out how sales of laptops and printers compare, for example, would be quite difficult if up-to-the-minute information was constantly changing the data in the database. This is the reason that analytical databases hold information *as of a specific point in time*.

Information that is as of a certain point in time is also called *a snapshot of data*. For example, if your analytical database holds a *snapshot* of sales information as of midnight each night, you will know that any day you look at the figures you will be seeing information as of midnight of the previous day. This way, daily, weekly, monthly or yearly comparison will make sense, since you will always have a consistent value with which to compare.

Analyzing data patterns and trends over time often requires large volumes of historical data. You may wish to analyze, for instance, how your customer base has been changing over time. Several years of data would be useful for such analysis, providing information on the demographics of your client base. Certainly, being aware that more women are buying computers and software than ever before, and understanding their buying patterns and trends would provide substantial information for changes in advertising and associated products. Another example may need twelve months of historical data to monitor sales volumes for the phase out of one product with the concurrent marketing and introduction of a comparable new product.

The idea that the data in an operational system is volatile and the data in an analytical system is nonvolatile directly relates to the different functionality of operational and analytical systems. The operational systems, which are running the daily business, have data that is changing constantly, as the previous inventory example indicates. This operational data is highly volatile. However, the data in the analytical database is a snapshot of data that will not change, as illustrated by the amount recorded as of midnight of the previous day.

Although data in an operational database may be changing throughout the day as business progresses, data in an analytical database will stay consistent and the database will be updated according to a pre-defined schedule.

An analytical database is most commonly designed as a *read-only database*. With a read-only database, users can look at the information, perhaps manipulate it in various ways on their desktops, but they can't change the value of the data in the database. A read-only database makes sense for analytical processing. Would you want the sales information as of a certain date to be changed at the discretion of the person in the department next to yours? Of course not. The only updates to the analytical database will be done according to its predefined schedule.

Another characteristic that distinguishes an operational system from an analytical system is the *design of the database*. An operational system is often designed to take in data, make changes to existing data, reconcile amounts, keep track of transactions, run reports, maintain data integrity, and manage transaction as quickly as possible. An analytical system is not designed to do any of those things. An analytical database is designed for large volumes of read-only data, providing information that will be used in making decisions. Thus, the design of an analytical database differs significantly from an operational database.

WHAT IS A DATA WAREHOUSE?

The concept of the data warehouse is often misunderstood. To minimize confusion, we have chosen to define a data warehouse as a read-only analytical database *that is used as the foundation of a decision support system.* Throughout the remainder of this book, the terms analytical database and data warehouse will be interchangeable and synonymous, having all of the characteristics we have thus far discussed. Below we will describe real life examples of data warehouses, their development lifecycles, and their uses.

REAL LIFE DATA WAREHOUSE EXAMPLES

Our first real life data warehouse is at Community Mutual Insurance Company. Community Mutual is a great example because its experiences in building and maintaining a data warehouse exhibit characteristics found in an overwhelming number of corporations that are building data warehouses. These shared characteristics include:

- The creation of predecessor systems that develop new skills and provide experience that directly transfers to the later development of the data warehouse.
- A user community that is spread across a continuum of sophisticated power users, mid-level users, and casual users.
- Ongoing decision support development.

Community Mutual also has two characteristics that are not as prevalent amidst corporations, but have added significantly to its success:

■ It had, and continues to have, strong sponsor support for development from the initial planning throughout its life cycle. This strong sponsorship for the data warehouse ensured continued support of the data warehouse as a high priority, strategic project.

■ Project managers and technical personnel responsible for providing information to clients/users have been working with the data warehouse since its beginning several years ago, and continue to do so through its various stages of change and development.

Community Mutual Insurance Company

A Corporate Overview. Community Mutual Insurance Company, an Ohio-based company, is a financially secure provider of quality health-care benefits. Serving over 2 million participants, Community Mutual was formed in 1984 as a result of the consolidation of Hospital Care Corporation, a Cincinnati-based Blue Cross licensee, and Ohio Medical Indemnity Mutual Corporation, a Blue Shield licensee based in Worthington, Ohio. Community Mutual has recently announced its intention to merge into Associated Insurance Companies, Inc., a transaction that is expected to be completed by the 4th quarter of 1995.

Over the past five years, Community Mutual has reorganized and developed a concise business strategy to reposition itself as a managed care company and to focus on its financial strength, diversification, marketing, organization, and operations. Community Mutual has developed a number of information management systems to support this business strategy, including a data warehouse for decision support.

Meeting the Need for Information—Predecessor Systems. The merger in 1984 required bringing together data from eighteen distinct systems for financial analysis. Community Mutual felt it was "drowning in data"; 90 percent of reporting analysis time was spent in collecting data from the various systems before analysis could be done. Customers and management wanted and needed more information, but analysts could provide only minimal information at a high cost within the desired timeframes.

In 1988 and 1989, Community Mutual designed the Corporate Financial & Statistical System, a predecessor to the data warehouse. Created to provide information and simplify reporting, it was a flat file extraction of selected corporate financial and statistical information. Batch SAS and COBOL programs were written against the file for reporting. Soon thereafter, a DB2 pilot project that extracted and summarized information was undertaken to do ad hoc reporting, but Community Mutual found that the table sizes (17+ million rows) made response times prohibitive for ad hoc reporting.

In a continuing effort to become more efficient so that more time could be spent on analyzing and producing valuable information for business decisions, plans for a data warehouse were developed. The data warehouse was started in October 1990 and took eighteen months to build.

The scope of the first project included the Financial and Actuarial subject areas, including claims, membership, and premium data. The source information was stored in flat files and IMS. A platform comparison project was done, with Teradata MPP becoming the target platform.

In the Beginning . . .   At its inception, the knowledge base of the developers on the data warehouse development team included limited experience with DB2, some data modeling, and a fairly strong knowledge of structured life cycle development techniques. At the beginning of development, in 1990, Community Mutual did not have specific front end tool expertise. Skill sets and tools specific to decision support processing were scarce.

Gathering Data Requirements.   Data requirements for the data warehouse were gathered through a series of Joint Application Development (JAD) sessions. Fast paced to get momentum moving, these JAD sessions were used to gather, organize, and order information requirements from multiple functional areas. Using their experience with structured methodologies, Community Mutual did process modeling first, decomposing functional areas and finding the decision support data useful for each high level process. This provided a clearer understanding for JAD attendees of the overlap in data between processes and how much of the desired data was the same (although called something different), and provided a forum for "if you could have any data, what would it be?"

The information gathered during requirements gathering was modeled using an entity relationship diagram (ERD). This was beneficial for presenting a pictorial way to represent the logical flow and relationships of the business. The initial JAD sessions were held for the Vice President and Director levels, with a second round for managers.

Infrastructures.   Infrastructures for the data warehouse were developed over the years as the project developed. No specific "infrastructure project" was undertaken to ascertain what structures to put into place. Rather, as technology and business requirements became apparent, appropriate structures were identified and implemented. For example, the business requirements of large volumes of detail accessible for timely ad hoc reporting was determined to require the power of an MPP platform, which in this case was Teradata. Like many other companies, Community Mutual moved from mainframe to a client/server environment. The introduction of LAN, gateways, communications, training, and front end tool infrastructures were driven by other projects. These infrastructures were then available for use in the data warehouse environment.

User Reaction to Initial Development.   The initial users of the Community Mutual data warehouse were a group of twenty to thirty business analysts who had been providing SAS reporting to the various business units inside the company. These were sophisticated users, who were used to the mainframe and data sets, knew the data, and took three days of SQL training. These users used a mainframe TSO screen, then logged into Teradata, which provided an on-line SQL and batch query capability.

Although the initial reaction to the data warehouse was quite positive, it took several months before even technical users began actively using the warehouse. The movement from standard reporting technologies using flat files to relational decision support technologies encompassed a broad learning curve. Additionally, the paradigm shift from high data acquisition time to high data analysis time was quite a jump. Few of the initial users had an understanding of the valuable processing power now available to them with the introduction of the data warehouse for decision support.

The User Community. Three distinctly different levels of users have emerged over the course of the last three years at Community Mutual. A similar user continuum has evolved in many organizations developing decision support systems, and requires thoughtful management and deployment of front end data access tools.

The levels of users at Community Mutual included:

- The power users (the technically sophisticated analysts described above).
- The mid-level users who develop ad hoc queries using parameters. These users were also trained on the data model. For this level of user, Community Mutual introduced GQL from Andyne Corporation, which allowed access to Teradata, thus bypassing the complexity of the mainframe for mid-level users.
- The novice or casual users, who are most comfortable in a point and click environment, where icons kick off predefined queries. Over the last few years, Visual Basic frontend applications were also developed and maintained to accommodate this level of user.

Currently, the data warehouse at Community Mutual has about 400 users, which is about 10 percent of the employees having access to the platform. It is available to every strategic business unit, and almost all the divisions within the Corporate Services Area use it.

Building on the Warehouse.   The first pass of the data warehouse covered 85 to 90 percent of their decision support data needs in 1992. Data was held at the detail level, which encompassed all of the components of a transaction. Development of the data warehouse included setting up a dedicated staff of Programmers, DBA's, System and Business Analysts, Training and User Support Personnel. Expansion of the warehouse has been ongoing and includes:

- Adding data from additional source systems
- Creating summarization tables to meet specific business needs
- Creating front-end data access applications
- Ongoing Training
- Establishing a help desk to assist users using the warehouse, as well as to provide a springboard for surfacing data integrity problems and resolutions. It was also used as a communication vehicle for user alerts, hardware down time, etc.
- Providing ongoing in-house marketing: A status report describing new capabilities within the data warehouse as well as new ideas for its use is published every month
- Forming a Data Warehouse Key Users Group to identify strategic issues and associated future data needs within the business units

What the Future Holds.   The decision support environment at Community Mutual continues to evolve. These are considered strategic systems having ongoing funding and support at the CEO level. Development over the next year includes:

- Reviewing the data transformation tools on the market to automate processing that is currently done with COBOL transformation programs.
- Modifying the methods of chargeback for data warehouse usage.
- Re-engineering the front end source systems and business models, and modifying subsequent sources for the warehouse.
- Modifying summary tables for re-engineered processes.
- Enhancing data warehouse administration.
- Modifying the logical and physical models for integrated health delivery systems.

20/20 Hindsight.   When reviewing the development and evolution of the data warehouse at Community Mutual, we asked the following questions:

1. What aspects of building the data warehouse were on track and went well?
   - Meeting the eighteen month timeline.
   - Using a dedicated development team.
   - User input in the development process.
   - Choice of target platform.
2. What would you do differently?
   - Put more emphasis on the difference between flat file and relational capabilities in the training program.
   - Market the capabilities of the data warehouse more actively.
   - Set better expectations of what the data warehouse can and cannot do.
   - Consider nationally recognized data naming and format standards.

3. Are there issues that must be continually tended to?
   - User training.
   - Data integrity.
   - Source system changes.
4. What advice would you give to another company that is just beginning its warehouse development?
   - Get support and involvement from your end user sponsor.

── *Tips from the Trenches 1.1* ──

LEARNING FROM COMMUNITY MUTUAL
INTERNAL COST ALLOCATIONS: CHARGEBACKS

1. Don't charge back on a usage basis. It inhibits use, explorations, and experimentation.

2. Depending on business unit acceptance, either allocate on a flat rate charge or no charge. One method to develop a flat rate charge is by using the business unit's proportion of data in the warehouse. The flat rate charge will help convert the business areas to using the new source because they will be paying twice—for their legacy system and the new warehouse. They can reduce their expense allocations by moving from their prior source files to the warehouse.

3. After an initial learning curve period (one to two years), to encourage efficient use of the warehouse, move to a combinaton of a flat charge, plus a variable charge based on utilization (cycles). The charge for utilization should be less than the flat charge because it is important to not inhibit experimentation and mining of the data.

A Consumer Packaged Goods Company

A Corporate Overview.   Our second example of a real life data warehouse is in a large consumer packaged goods company, which we will call the CPG Company. A classical organization structure is in place within the company, where the market research group is responsible for acquisition and analysis of syndicated data sources. The marketing and sales departments were recipients of this data and analysis.

How it Got Started.   The marketing research department had been reviewing the marketplace for end user decision support tools for some time. The IS organization saw the need to support the analysis of internal shipments and syndicated data and became involved in the process. The organization decided to get a good understanding of how a decision support tool could bring business value to the corporation. After reviewing a variety of alternatives, the group decided to do a hands on evaluation of the Data Interpretation System (DIS) from Metaphor, Incorporated.[2]

The evaluation process began at the end of 1990. Sample syndicated data was manually transformed into a star database structure, and loaded into a relational database at Metaphor. The CPG Company provided analysts to work with the Metaphor team, so they learned firsthand the drawbacks and the benefits of the system. The project team then presented its results to key sponsors from market research, marketing, and sales. The recommendation to move forward with the technology was approved. This was the first data warehouse/decision support initiative within this organization.

Implementation Project.   The initial project team was comprised of both customer and vendor staff. The development plans called for implementation of both syndicated scanner and internal shipments data. The project was phased to load data for one division at a time. The primary purpose of including vendor consultants on the project team was to ensure extensive skills transfer into the client organization.

The decision support requirements were defined through an interview process much like that described in Chapter 6. Formal data modeling was not done, but data requirements were translated directly into a star database design.

Purchased data was received on tape from the data vendor. The CPG Company sent several people to a workshop specifically to understand techniques to efficiently transform raw data into data warehouse structures. The data was then extracted, transformed, and loaded into DB2 by the client programming staff. A starter set of applications was developed using the DIS tool.

Architecture and Infrastructure.   Due to the nature of the Metaphor product, DIS, many of the challenges associated with setting up a data warehouse and architecture were minimized. The DIS product architecture included a file server, LAN, database gateways, LAN-to-LAN routing, complete end user tool set including data access, statistical analysis, word processing, spreadsheets, graphing, and e-mail. This complete infrastructure provided a stable and mature environment to support high-powered analysis.

It is important to put the data warehouse development process at the CPG Company into perspective. Metaphor provided comprehensive architecture and infrastructure for decision support processing. This eliminated the need for the client company to purchase, install, be trained on, and integrate multiple new technologies. This enabled the organization to focus all of its efforts on the database and end user application development. The message from this example is, as you begin the data warehouse development process, don't underestimate the effort required to build up the complete infrastructure to support a data warehouse.

Over the past several years, the CPG Company has implemented other workgroup and personal productivity tools. The next generation of data warehouse access will leverage the investment already in place for other purposes. Again, the data warehouse initiatives are not burdened with the task of implementing wide-scale client server architectures, but can focus on the database and the front end data access.

End User Reaction.   The CPG Company did a superb job in managing expectations and marketing the project internally. Key activities included:

- Setting clear project goals to help manage user expectations for access.
- Giving presentations about the data warehouse, its data, what it could do for users.
- Demonstrating the proof of concept and then the live warehouse.
- Meeting with users every other week after training to discuss using the data warehouse.
- Presenting giveaways printed with the project logo.
- Publicizing successes across the entire organization.

Each division had a different strategy to encourage use of the warehouse. Some divisions included tool proficiency in the job description and performance criteria for market research analysts; other groups did not. Upon initial implementation, the marketing users took the lead from the marketing research analysts to begin building their own analyses. Where the analysts became extremely adept with the tool, more benefits were derived from the data warehouse immediately and over time.

Four years later a review of the data warehouse and tool use showed the impact of putting incentives in place. The departments that institutionalized the use of the warehouse had developed a much larger library of analyses and had maintained a high level of expertise. The groups that set forth job responsibilities ensured continued expertise over time when the original user base had moved on.

Data Warehouse Expansion.   After the data for the initial department was implemented, the internal team went on to include all other departments/divisions. Over time, other related data sources have been added to support market research, marketing, and sales.

The dissolution of Metaphor has forced the organization to rethink its tools strategy. There are multiple threads of activity. For the remote sales force, a Windows-based access tool was implemented using the existing data warehouse structures. For expansion of the data warehouse into other business functions, a review of the tools marketplace was again initiated. At this time, the CPG Company is in the process of developing an enterprise-wide strategy for expanding the warehouse and DSS Agent from MicroStrategy will be used as the front end of choice for the next phases of the data warehouse growth.

20/20 Hindsight.   In retrospect, several key decisions were made to ensure the success of the data warehouse development at the CPG Company:

- Solid corporate commitment to making the project successful.
- Both end user and IS management support.
- Necessary resources put in place to make the development project work.
- A realistic assessment of available skill sets. Hire when necessary, but apply internal resources so that skills transfer occurs.
- Focus on cultural changes and address the issues head on.

Bottom line: investments in a data warehouse and decision support system are well worth it!

SUMMARY

In this chapter, you should have learned the following:

- A decision support sytem provides information to assist employees in making decisions and more effectively doing their jobs.
- Decision support systems can be used for short-term tactical decision making, such as the movement of inventory on a weekly basis, or for long-term strategic decision making, such as the introduction of a product or service into a new market.
- Operational systems are systems which run the data-to-day business of a company.
- Analytical databases provide information that is used for analyzing a problem or situation. Analytical processing is primarily done through comparisons, or by analyzing patterns and trends.
- Analytical databases do not hold up-to-the-minute information, but hold information as of a specific point in time. This is also called a snapshot of data.
- Analytical databases are often quite large because analyzing patterns and trends often requires large volumes of historical data.
- Analytical databases are usually read-only. They cannot be updated on-line by users, and will only be updated systematically, according to a predefined schedule.
- A data warehouse is an analytical database that is used as the foundation of a decision support system.

ENDNOTES

1. Knowledge about the characteristics of analytical databases is becoming more common in business today. We would, however,

like to acknowledge William H. Inmon, President of Prism Solutions, Inc., for his pioneering efforts in disseminating these ideas.

2. Metaphor, Incorporated, founded in 1982, was purchased by IBM as a wholly owned and independently managed subsidiary in 1991. Responsibility for the DIS product was integrated into the core IBM organization and the separate subsidiary was dissolved as of October 1994. DIS is no longer being actively marketed by IBM.

Chapter 2

Understanding Terms and Technology

There are a number of new terms and technologies for developers to understand when embarking on their first decision support project. This chapter will define those that are pertinent to the development of a data warehouse for decision support. Some of the terms have entire chapters devoted to them; others are more common terms used throughout the book. This chapter will provide an overview of key concepts used in the remainder of this book.

ANALYTICAL PROCESSING

Analytical processing (also called informational or decision support processing) is processing done to support strategic and management decision making. Data used in analytical processing is often historical in nature, permitting users to analyze trends and patterns with a large amount of data over wide ranges of time. Analytical processing systems are customarily read only and do not permit the data to be updated by users as do operational systems.

OPERATIONAL PROCESSING

Operational processing refers to systems that run the day-to-day business for companies. The emphasis of these systems is to support business functionality by processing transactions accurately and efficiently. Common examples of this type of processing are order entry, manufacturing scheduling, and general ledger.

DECISION SUPPORT SYSTEMS

A *decision support system* is a system which provides information to users so that they can analyze a situation and make decisions. Put another way, a decision support system provides information to assist employees in making decisions and more effectively doing their jobs. This decision making can be long-term strategic decision making, such as analyzing buying patterns over several years to develop a new product or service, or perhaps to introduce a product into a new European or Far Eastern location. Decision making could also be short term and tactical in nature, such as reviewing and changing recommended order quantities for a particular product.

DATA WAREHOUSE

A *data warehouse* is an analytical database that is used as the foundation of a decision support system. It is designed for large volumes of read-only data, providing intuitive access to information that will be used in making decisions.

ENVIRONMENT FOR DATA ACCESS

In the world of data warehousing, the *environment for data access* includes the front end data access tools and technologies allowing users to easily access the data, the training that must take place for users to use these tools and technologies, the implementation of metadata, and the training to navigate through the metadata.

ARCHITECTURE

An *architecture* is a set of rules or structures providing a framework for the overall design of a system or product. There are networking architectures, client-server architectures, architectures for specific products, as well as many others. Figure 2–1 illustrates a client-server architecture with data on the server. A *data architecture* provides this framework by identifying and understanding how the data will move throughout the system and be utilized within the corporation. The *data architecture for a data warehouse* has as a primary component a read-only data-

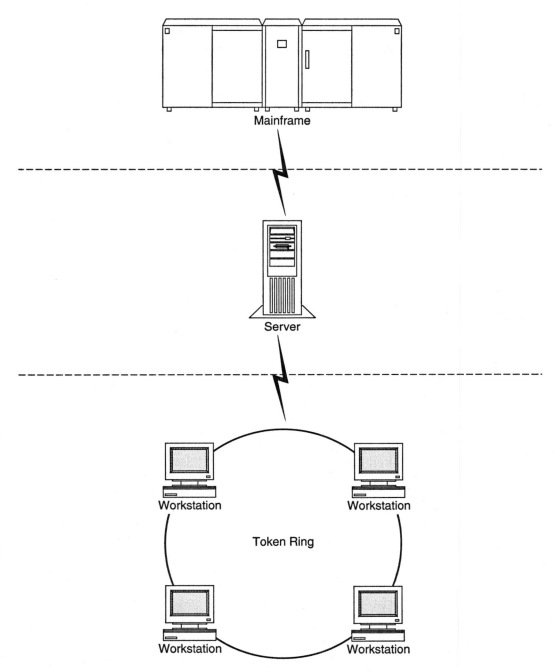

FIGURE 2–1. One example of a three-tier architecture.

base used for decision support. Figure 2–2 shows one possible data warehouse data architecture.

TECHNICAL INFRASTRUCTURES

Technical infrastructures are closely related to architecture and are the technologies, platforms, databases, gateways, and other components necessary to make the architecture functional within the corporation. See Figure 2–3 for examples of technical infrastructures. For the purposes of this book, technical training is also considered a technical infrastructure.

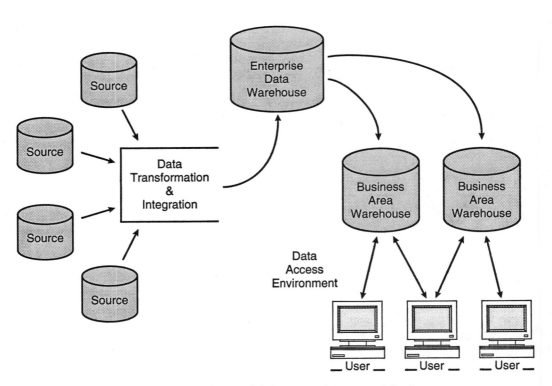

FIGURE 2–2.   One valid data warehouse architecture.

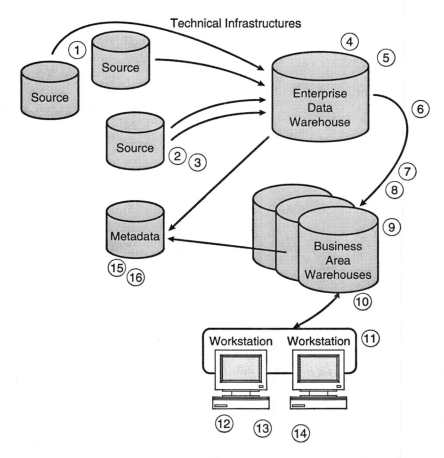

1. Decision Support Education
2. Data Transformation Tool Selection
3. Data Transformation Tool Training
4. Database, Platforms in Place
5. Database, Platform Expertise
6. Gateway Selection
7. Data Replication Strategies
8. Replication Tool Selection
9. Expertise in Data Warehouse Database Design
10. Database, Platforms in Place
11. Network, Communications in Place
12. Workstations, Software Installed
13. Data Access Tool Selection
14. Data Access User Training
15. Metadata Access
16. Metadata Navigation Training

FIGURE 2–3. Example of technical infrastructures in a data warehouse architecture.

SOURCE AND TARGET DATA

Source data is the data in the different databases, files, segments, and so on, that will be extracted from the operational (day-to-day processing) systems. Source data can also come from outside the corporation through, for instance, companies specializing in providing data to corporations. The *target data* is the data that goes into the fields within the data warehouse database. For example, the source data may be your current IMS, DB2, and VSAM operational data, while your target may be DB2 (or any other relational or multidimensional database being used for your data warehouse) (see Figure 2–4).

LEVELS OF USERS

There is a broad spectrum of different types of end users who will use a data warehouse. The first level of user, called a *novice* or *casual user*, is someone who needs access to information on an occasional basis, and who will not be logged on daily, or in some cases even weekly. Most often, big button navigation and prompting of choices for predefined analysis is appropriate for the casual user.

Business analysts, the largest group of users, use information daily, but do not have (and don't necessarily want to have) the technical knowledge to build reports completely from scratch. These users will want predefined navigation paths, the ability to customize reports, and will look at reports in a variety of different ways.

Every organization has some business professionals who are *power users*. This type of user will want to write their own macros, change parameters, and manipulate result sets. These users are also comfortable starting with a clean slate and creating their own reports/analyses.

The final level of user is the *application developer*. Usually, the application developer's primary responsibilities are to support the business, rather than having other actual business re-

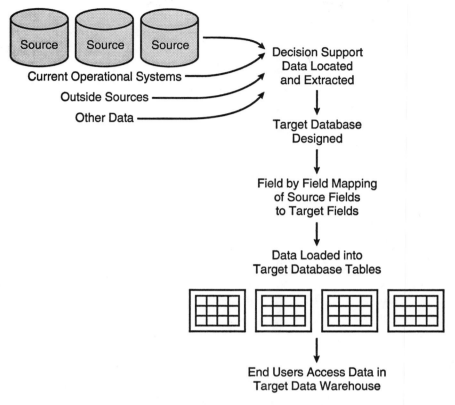

FIGURE 2–4.   Source and target data.

sponsibilities also. The application developer will be trained to not only create reports/analyses for use by others but will be a driving force in setting standards, and identifying where and how reports will be named and located.

CLASSES OF TOOLS

Data access/query tools provide a graphical user interface to the data warehouse. The user will interact directly with the table structures, sometimes with a layer of abstraction to allow him or her to assign business names to the different tables and columns.

Report writers may also provide a layer of abstraction that allows the assigning of business names to the different columns and tables. These tools provide extensive formatting capabilities to allow the re-creation of a report to look a specific way. Again, users tend to have to work closely with the physical table structures.

Multidimensional database management systems (MDBMS) provide advanced metric support with extensive slice and dice capabilities.

Advanced decision support tools provide advanced multidimensional analysis directly against the relational database management system. These tools are often driven off of shared metadata and support advanced metrics, extensive slice and dice, and drilling capabilities.

Executive information systems (EIS) provide a structured, big button interface to predefined reports that provide highly summarized topline information about the business.

DECISION SUPPORT SYSTEM (DSS) APPLICATIONS

A *DSS application* is a collection of one or more predefined reports or analyses. These are developed in advance by an application developer or a power user. A specific predefined report can generate hundreds of unique variations simply by changing the constraints. These applications are usually developed using powerful data access tools rather than a third- or fourth-generation language.

DATA TRANSFORMATION

Within the data warehouse environment, *data transformation* is processing that is done on data to change its characteristics. Typically, data transformation is done when data is extracted from the operational systems and may encompass integrating dissimilar data types, changing codes (i.e., changing male and female from 1,2 to M, F), and selectively choosing data using if . . . else, if . . . then, and similar constructs. Data transformation also includes processing to do calculations, summarize data, and to reconcile disparate update cycles. Most transformation tools generate the code to do the data transformations.

DATA TRANSFORMATION TOOLS

Data transformation tools are software designed to automate the process of extracting data from heterogeneous (dissimilar) sources (databases, files, segments, etc.), mapping the source data to target data, creating DDL (data definition language), generating the code to transform or manipulate the data, and loading the data into the target database. Some transformation tools have all of these features, some do not. Others, in addition, have the capacity to update the new target database on a scheduled basis. Figure 2–5 explains the general functionality of transformation technology.

MIDDLEWARE TOOLS

Due to confusion surrounding the definition of this term in the marketplace, it will generally not be used in this book. Instead, the term Data Transformation tools is used, with the above definition.

METADATA

Metadata is "data about data" and provides information about the data structures and the relationships between the data structures within or between databases. In a data warehouse environment, there are two types of metadata of interest. The first is metadata for the operational systems to the data ware-

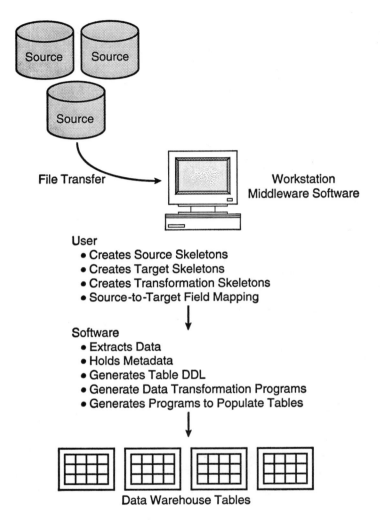

FIGURE 2–5.   Generic Data Transformation functionality.

house and may encompass the original source system name, data types and any source to target transformations. The second type of metadata maps data from the warehouse to the end user's Dimensional Business Model and front end tool and will usually include business names and hierarchies. This type of metadata, often called DSS metadata, also drives application development for advanced decision support tools.

STAR SCHEMA

A *star schema* is a specific type of database design used to support analytical processing. It has a specific set of normalized tables. A star schema contains two types of tables, *fact tables* and *dimension tables*. Fact tables, sometimes called major tables, contain the quantitative or factual data about a business—the information being queried. This information is often numerical measurements and can consist of many columns and millions of rows. Dimension tables, sometimes called minor tables, are smaller and hold descriptive data that reflect the dimensions of a business. SQL queries then use predefined and user-defined join paths between fact and dimension tables, with constraints on the data to return selected information.

HIERARCHIES

Business *hierarchies* describe organizational structure and logical parent child relationships within the data. An example would be store to district to region structures for managing a retail business.

GRANULARITY

Granularity is the level of detail within the data warehouse and is one of the principal design issues in data warehouse development. Highly granular data provides a great deal of detailed information and subsequently a large volume of data. For instance, a high granularity level can provide a list of all the transactions in your checking account for the month, and could answer the question, "Was there a debit to my account on June 5th? Less granular data provides less detailed data, more levels of summary, and less data volume. Coarser data would not have that level of detail available, but can provide an answer to "What were the monthly (or yearly) balances on my account for the last 3 years? (given the information for three years was available). Granularity levels directly affect the size of the database and the types of analysis that the database can support.

DATABASE GATEWAY

A *database gateway* is a product that allows data to pass smoothly between heterogeneous (dissimilar) databases or systems. Gateways can involve connections between different networks, different communications protocols, and different representations of data. For example, in the data warehouse environment where much of the legacy data resides on a mainframe, a gateway provides the connectivity required to access data from the mainframe to be used with other types of databases running on a different operating system.

MEGABYTES, GIGABYTES, AND TERABYTES

A *megabyte (MB)* is a unit of measurement of computer memory or data storage capacity equal to 1,048,576 bytes. A *gigabyte (GB)* equals 1,073,741,824 bytes or 1,024 megabytes. A *terabyte (TB)* equals 1,099,511,627,776 bytes or 1,024 gigabytes. Chances are you won't get higher than terabytes, at least this time around!

DECISION SUPPORT DEVELOPMENT CYCLE

The life cycle of decision support system development which includes the following phases: planning, gathering data requirements and modeling, physical database design and development, data mapping and transformation, data extraction and load, automating the data management process, application development—creating the starter set of reports, data validation and testing, training, and rollout.

SUMMARY

In this chapter, you should have learned the following:

■ Data warehouse and decision support related definitions that provide many of the underlying concepts necessary to understand the remainder of this book.

Chapter 3

Understanding Architecture and Infrastructures

THE TASK AT HAND

Setting the Scene: A recent, well publicized change in corporate direction has put a strong focus on customer profiling and market segmentation within your corporation. In an effort to get the customer information to the people who need it, a data warehouse is being developed. You have been assigned as the project manager, and tasked with building a data warehouse for the marketing department of your multimillion dollar company.

The programmer in the cubicle next to yours says "What's the big deal? All you have to do is put the data into a different database and slap an easy-to-use front end on it."

You find out the actuarial department has its own small "data warehouse" they created last year that has a great front end. In fact, they use it in client presentations to show how easily they can get information on any client account at the click of a mouse!

You know there is no enterprise data model in the corporation. Everything you read says to start from the enterprise data model. Will you have to go through all the work of creating an enterprise data model to build the warehouse?

In a conversation about decision support systems, you are shocked when someone from the database group says, "We've got half a dozen different decision support systems in production right now."

Talking with the coworker responsible for the recent corporate-wide front end tool survey, you find out there are dozens of companies marketing their products as the data warehouse front end solution.

A division in New York has developed several warehouses that do both decision support and on-line transaction processing.

Telephone calls to different companies elicit the following facts: One company has been developing its data warehouse for the last three years, with the initial development taking fifteen months. They now have 200 people using it on a daily basis. Another company built its data warehouse in three months, and are starting their second version now. Both companies had at least one unsuccessful attempt at building a data warehouse.

Confused yet about all the different ideas, opinions, definitions, and products associated with building a data warehouse? Is it possible that one company took three months and another took fifteen months to build a warehouse? Why such a disparity? What, exactly, is going on here?

UNDERSTANDING DATA WAREHOUSE ARCHITECTURE

The first step in clarifying some of the misunderstandings surrounding the data warehouse is understanding data warehouse architecture. Let's review the definition of architecture. An *architecture* is a set of rules or structures providing a framework for the overall design of a system or product. There are networking architectures, client-server architectures, architectures for specific products, as well as many others. A *data architecture* provides a framework by identifying and understanding how data will move throughout the system and be utilized within the corporation. A *data warehouse architecture* has as a primary component a read-only database used for decision support.

An architecture, then, is the framework made up of rules or structures that the system will be built upon. The architecture for a data warehouse has its own characteristics that differentiate it from other systems.

THE CHARACTERISTICS OF DATA WAREHOUSE ARCHITECTURE

The basic architecture for a data warehouse is shown in Figure 3–1.

The distinguishing characteristics of data warehouse architecture are:

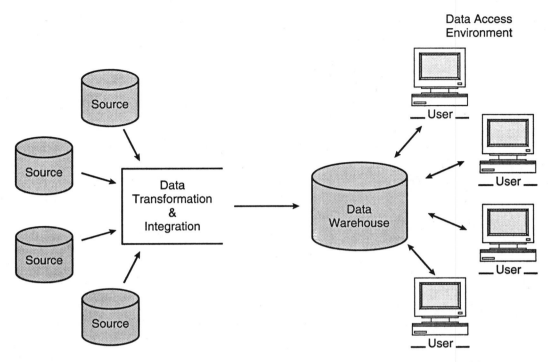

FIGURE 3–1.   Data warehouse architectures: Generic data warehouse architecture.

■ Data is extracted from source systems, databases, and files.

■ The data from the source systems is integrated and transformed before being loaded into the data warehouse.

■ The data warehouse is a separate read-only database created specifically for decision support.

■ Users access the data warehouse via a front end tool or application.

Data Is Extracted from Source Systems, Database, or Files

The legacy systems within the company are customarily the predominant source of data for the data warehouse. Data fields identified as necessary for decision support processing will be extracted from these systems. Often, this may entail extracting specific data fields from many different systems, databases or files. Sometimes entire files may be extracted, if all the fields are necessary for decision support processing.

Other sources of data may be data that is bought from companies specializing in providing data, such as Metro Mail, A.C. Nielsen, or IRI. These sources of data may be in a variety of formats and on different mediums, so selective field extraction from the files may or may not be necessary.

In general, it is quite common within a data warehouse architecture for the data sources to be from multiple systems or applications. Source fields may come from different databases, different platforms, and in a variety of data types and formats.

The Data from the Source Systems Is Integrated and Transformed before Being Loaded into the Data Warehouse

A significant component of data warehouse architecture is that the data from multiple sources is integrated and/or transformed before being loaded into the data warehouse. This is an important and often side-stepped characteristic of a data warehouse. If data is coming from multiple systems, databases, and platforms, some form of data integration or transformation will be necessary. For example, the Product Number being held in several different systems, in many corporations, has several different formats and sizes. In one system (within the same company) it may be a 9-digit code, in another an 11-digit field, while the third system automatically appends a product category code on the end for reporting purposes. Sound familiar? Of course it does, because there is a good chance these are the same types of data inconsistencies you are trying to deal with in your own corporate databases and applications.

In many companies, keys in existing systems have intelligence built into the format. This is a very common practice in the design of operational systems that must be transformed before being loaded into a data warehouse. For example, Product Number has codes built into the format (Figure 3–2).

Keys with intelligent codes built in that have not been transformed present decision support report challenges. For instance, using Figure 3–2, with no data transformation being done, how would you compare sales on all of the products for specific sales territories within a region? The majority of the data warehouses will be either relational or multidimensional database technology. They are accessed with SQL or a multidimensional querying language, neither of which lend themselves easily to queries to pull embedded knowledge out of a data structure.

To do reporting on the sales of all products for certain territories within a region, a cross reference/data transformation algorithm would be established to transform the data in the Product Number field from the different source systems. This algorithm could map the source data to several different relational fields in the data warehouse database and will make the actual Product Number a consistent data type and format. This is an example of the type of data transformation often needed in a data warehouse. Within the data warehouse architecture, data is transformed and/or integrated before being loaded into the data warehouse database.

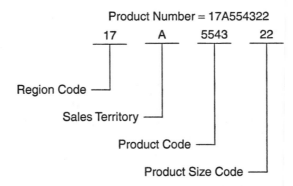

FIGURE 3–2. A field with codes built into the key.

A Separate Read-only Database Is Created for Decision Support Data

The operative words here are "separate" and "read-only." Inherent in the data warehouse architecture is the idea that operational and decision support processing is fundamentally different. Operational processing is running the day-to-day business operations of the corporation. Operational systems are often on-line transaction systems that take in, update, and store the core data that is running the corporate business systems. Decision support processing is providing, in an easy-to-understand format, analytical information to assist in making tactical and strategic business decisions within the corporation. These decision-making processes often require a range of historical data that is used for comparative analysis, and allow for monitoring trends and information patterns over time. The fundamental differences in functionality of operational and decision support systems require substantially different styles of database design. Operational databases are designed to store, update, and report on day-to-day business data with speed while decision support systems are designed to provide easy access to read-only historical and analytical information. One database design cannot efficiently provide both types of functionality. Hence, the separate read-only database is a primary component of the data warehouse architecture.

Users Access the Data Warehouse via a Front End Tool or Application

In most data warehouse systems, the data access environment makes up the next layer of the data warehouse architecture. This data access environment is comprised of the front end tools, applications, training, and support necessary to provide useful and accessible decision support information from the data warehouse. In many cases, the core technologies for data access will be within a client-server environment, with the workstation as the client and the data warehouse as the server. There are, however, many variations of data access being used as more data warehouses are being implemented. The issues associated with the data access environment, the importance of the front end, and lack of knowledge about analytical analysis for decision support will be discussed extensively in Chapter 8. The data warehouse architecture will always include the data access environment that provides front end data access to the users of the decision support data.

EXPANDING THE GENERIC DATA WAREHOUSE ARCHITECTURE

The data warehouse architecture described thus far contains the components which distinguish the data warehouse. This is considered a *generic data warehouse architecture.* Part of the task of building a data warehouse is to incorporate the primary constructs of the generic data warehouse architecture into your current systems architecture to fulfill your decision support processing needs.

It is important to understand that the constructs of the generic data warehouse architecture can be implemented within corporations in very sophisticated ways. A review of some data warehouse architectures that are currently being implemented in different companies will explain some variations on the generic data warehouse theme. For the first example, refer to Figure 3–3.

Figure 3–3 is a data warehouse architecture in which an Enterprise Data Warehouse is loading data to Business Area Warehouses. Why would a corporation implement this type of architecture for a data warehouse? There may be several reasons:

■ To fulfill a strategic initiative requirement that all databases use the Enterprise Data Model as their base.

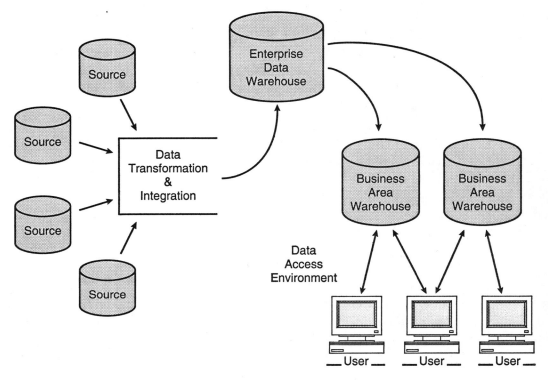

FIGURE 3–3.   Data warehouse architectures: Enterprise warehouse feeding business area warehouses.

- ■ To separate the processes of source data transformation/ integration from processes of database design and denormalization.

- ■ To use the Enterprise Data Warehouse as a consistent source for all source-to-target mappings for multiple Business Area Warehouses.

The integration of a data warehouse architecture into your current systems architecture is not always as straightforward and simple as you would initially think. Current data processing system architectures are extremely sophisticated at some corporations (both by design and lack of design). In most corporations, there will be some type of constraints set in implementing the data warehouse architecture. These constraints can be a variety of technical, integration, strategic, or political considerations that introduce limitations as to how the data warehouse architecture can be implemented within your corporation.

Since an architecture is a set of rules or structures providing a framework for the overall design of a system or product, it cannot be separated from the data warehouse itself. The implementation of data warehouse architecture can be done in a variety of ways, and can become quite complicated within a corporation. However, the basic constructs of the data warehouse architecture must be put into place. There is no right way to implement a data warehouse architecture. However, there are certain structures that must be in place. Additionally, there are different technical solutions in response to different corporate environments, constraints, and requirements.

In our example in Figure 3–3, the basic data warehouse architecture constructs are in place. Data is extracted from source systems, databases, and files. The data from the source systems is integrated and transformed before being loaded into the read-only Enterprise Data Warehouse. This data is then restructured, redesigned, and loaded into separate read-only Business Area Warehouses, which are used for decision support processing. Users access the data warehouse via a front end tool or application. This is indeed a data warehouse architecture that has been modified to accommodate the strategic initiatives, the decision support requirements, and technical constraints of the company.

Part of building a data warehouse is a process of finding the correct technical solution to your decision support needs and creating a solid data warehouse architecture within the parameters you have to work with. One architecture is not better than another. Certainly, one architecture may be more difficult or time consuming to develop than another. In most cases however, the chosen data warehouse architecture implementation is the most appropriate technical solution based on the corporation's goals, architecture constraints, and decision support requirements.

Another data warehouse architecture implementation is shown in Figure 3–4.

Figure 3–4 shows a data warehouse architecture in which the data is transformed and redesigned, and then loaded into separate Business Area Warehouses. Although this data warehouse architecture does not have one large database, it has all of the constructs that qualify it as a true data warehouse. Perhaps there are constraints associated with database size that this architecture implementation is accommodating.

Another real-life data warehouse architecture implementation is shown in Figure 3–5.

Figure 3–5 is quite a sophisticated architecture in which

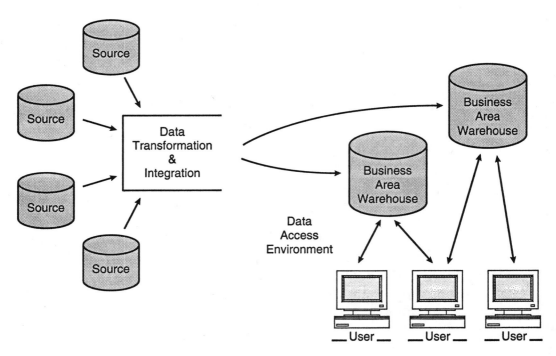

FIGURE 3–4. Data warehouse architectures: Subject area warehouses.

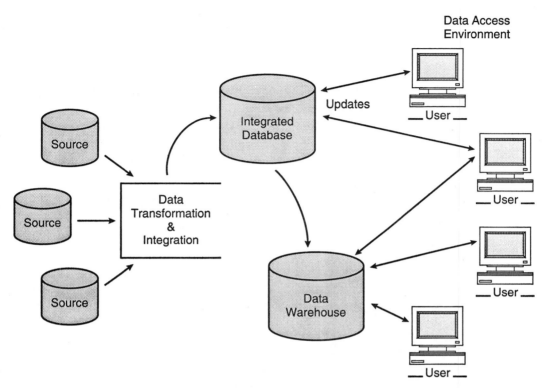

FIGURE 3–5.   Data warehouse architectures: Integrated database feeding
a data warehouse.

data is extracted from the source systems, goes through data
transformation and integration and is loaded into an integrated
relational database, which is designed in third normal form.
The information that is loaded into the integrated database is
read-only. New data is also being added to the database as new
data fields needed for decision support are being populated by
users. Why would a corporation use this architecture? This
company realized they needed integrated data to make their
daily business decisions because it was just too time and error
intensive trying to get information from hundreds of applications. The issue of providing valuable, integrated information

for running the business was the first priority. Cleaning up and adding additional fields to the database was part of this process. Now this company is moving forward with a data warehouse for long-term strategic business decisions.

Using our definition of data warehouse architecture, is the integrated database shown in Figure 3–5, which is being used for daily tactical decision making, a data warehouse? Absolutely not. It does not have one of the primary components of the data warehouse architecture: A read-only database. Nor, by the way, was it designed for decision support processing. However, the data warehouse itself has the primary characteristics of the data warehouse architecture.

There are several options for loading the data warehouse in this architecture. One option would be to load the data from the integrated database, knowing that the data has been through the cleansing and data transformation process. The integrated database is in third normal form, so data loaded into the data warehouse would require redesign to process decision support information effectively. Because this data had parts that were read-only and other new fields were entered by users, data cleansing programs would need to be part of the data transformation process to handle user input errors before being loaded into the data warehouse.

UNDERSTANDING THE RELATIONSHIP OF INFRASTRUCTURES AND ARCHITECTURE

Technical infrastructures are closely related to architecture and are the technologies, platforms, databases, gateways, and other components necessary to support the chosen data warehouse architecture. For the purposes of this book, technical training is also considered a technical infrastructure. For example, technical infrastructures may include the choice and installation of the database, setting up the network, or choosing and installing the front end tools. The architecture is a set of rules or structures that create a framework for development and implementation of a data warehouse. The technical infrastructures are the components that need to be in place for that architecture to perform.

Architecture and infrastructures are closely related. However, the same architecture may require different infrastructures depending upon the particular corporate environment. The following figures show the same data warehouse architecture being implemented using different infrastructures. Figure 3–6 shows the generic data warehouse architecture. Figures 3–7 and 3–8 show how the same architecture could be implemented with different infrastructures depending on the corporate environment, decision support needs, and system architecture.

In Figure 3–7, the company is a specialty insurance com-

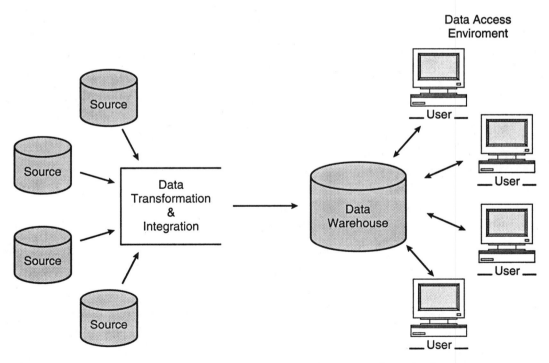

FIGURE 3–6.   Data warehouse architectures: Generic data warehouse architecture.

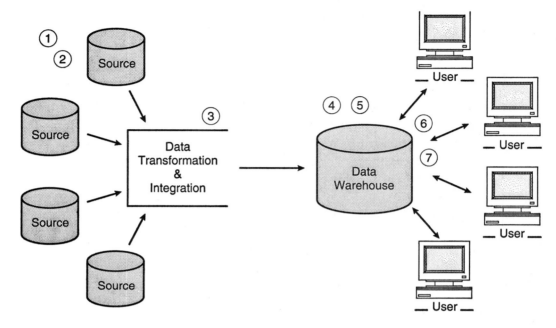

FIGURE 3–7.   The relationship of architecture and infrastructures.

pany that is building its first data warehouse. The source data is VSAM files off of the mainframe, the data warehouse target database is a relational database. Front end tools are being used on workstations to provide data access to the new data warehouse. Figure 3–7 shows some of the infrastructures this company will implement to fulfill the goal of providing decision support information to its users.

The infrastructures for Figure 3–7 may be:

1. *Training in decision support technology.* Training in decision support technology will describe what a data warehouse is, what it is used for, and how it is built. This is a necessary infrastructure for this company, which has no experience in decision support systems development. The audience will be the development project team.

2. *Training in relational database technology.* This company has always been a COBOL shop and has not yet had a reason to move into relational technology. The data warehouse will be its first attempt at building a relational system. Relational database training would be an important infrastructure at this company. A clear understanding of relational database design and the design characteristics particular to decision support processing will also be necessary.

3. *Data transformation and integration.* Data transformation and integration is being done programmatically and no data transformation tools will be bought to automate this process.

4. *DBA skills* A consultant is being hired to assist the company in relational database design and administration. He or she will also act as a mentor to an in-house employee to insure database knowledge is transferred to the company.

5. *The hardware and relational database are already purchased and the software is loaded.* This infrastructure is already in place.

6. *The local area network, communications, and workstations are set up.* This infrastructure is already in place.

7. *Gateway products are being reviewed for purchase.* The purchase, installation, and testing of the gateway is an infrastructure.

8. *Front end software is being reviewed.* The original list of fifteen front end products is now down to three products that have been identified by the users as options for data warehouse data access. Software purchases, installation, and training will be an infrastructure.

9. *Metadata navigation tools are being reviewed.* This infrastructure is being done in association with 8 above. Some front end tools provide metadata navigation functionality; many do not. A review of metadata tools enabling users to navigate through the data warehouse and understand the location and structure of the data is an important infrastructure.

As you can see, infrastructures are the software, the hardware, the training, and all of the other components providing the necessary support for the implementation of a data warehouse architecture. One aspect of developing a data warehouse in an architected environment is to take the time to find the best data warehouse data architecture for your particular environment. Another fundamental aspect of building a successful data warehouse is to identify the infrastructures that will be necessary to implement this chosen architecture.

In the next example, Figure 3–8, the same architecture is being implemented amidst different infrastructures. The source of data is DB2, IMS, VSAM, and an outside source. The target database is Sybase. Let's look at those infrastructures.

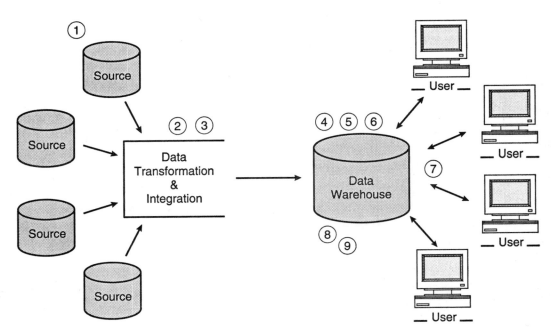

FIGURE 3–8.   Same architecture, different infrastructures.

1. *Training in decision support technology.* Training in decision support technology will describe what a data warehouse is, what it is used for, and how it is built. This is a necessary infrastructure for this company, which has no experience in decision support systems development. The audience will be the development project team.

2. *Transformation tool choice, purchase, and installation.* The transformation tool was chosen as part of a corporate-wide data architecture and infrastructure project. It is viewed as a strategic tool that will benefit several conversion or client-server projects being done within the company.

3. *Transformation tool vendor training.* A three-day training course will provide the basic formation necessary to make this tool useable in the corporate environment. Extra time is then added to the project plan to accommodate the learning curve as technicians get up to speed on the tool.

4. *New hardware and a new relational database has been chosen and installed.*

5. *Database administration and Unix training has been scheduled.* This is an important infrastructure to begin to build a knowledge base on a new relational database, database-specific SQL and in Unix.

6. *DBA skills.* A consultant is being hired to assist the company in transferring current relational database knowledge to the new relational database. He or she will act as a mentor to the current DBAs about issues particular to the new database.

7. The front end has been chosen. An advanced decision support tool has been chosen, and an application developer has been trained on the tool.

8. *Unix job-scheduling software.* Job-scheduling software has been located, purchased, and installed. In addition, two weeks

of vendor consulting has been purchased so the client site understands how to set up the scheduling process.

9. *Metadata access.* The metadata will be accessed via the company's new repository product. A separate project will be established to populate the repository, define procedures, and develop the necessary user training for metadata navigation.

You can see that the infrastructures for the two corporations as depicted in Figures 3–7 and 3–8 are very different, although the architecture is the same. Timelines and budgets to implement these architectures and infrastructures could be significantly different. The first example is a bit simpler, easier to set up, and may be less costly.

ARCHITECTURE AND INFRASTRUCTURES AS A SEPARATE PROJECT

It is highly recommended that identifying data warehouse architecture and infrastructures be a separate project from the actual development of the data warehouse. It is not necessary to take a great deal of time working through the technical considerations necessary to understand the proper (or best choice) architecture for warehouse development. With some focused attention, recommendations on architecture and infrastructures can be done fairly quickly.

It is not a good idea, however, to mix the analysis necessary for creating a solid data warehouse architecture into your data warehouse development project plan. Doing so may draw out your decision support development timelines to unacceptable dates. For example, how long will it take to get a specific piece of hardware purchased and installed? How about agreement on a front end or data transformation tool? Many companies do not have corporate structures that provide quick and easy mechanisms for making these types of decisions.

Tips from the Trenches 3.1 ———

ARCHITECTURE AND INFRASTRUCTURES

1. First, clarify what it is you are building. Is this truly a data warehouse or is it an integrated database or repository?

2. Figure out the architecture and infrastructures *before* beginning your warehouse development project.

3. Always look at data warehouse architecture from a corporate-wide level. Do a little investigative work if you hear the words "repository, data warehouse, decision support, integrated database."

4. Don't pretend that the development team will just know how to build a data warehouse for decision support processing. Get training in decision support technologies and database design. It is necessary to make a paradigm shift from operational to decision support thinking, and training in decision support concepts is an important step in that process.

5. Work quickly through the architecture and infrastructure phase. If there are aspects that can't be figured out right now, acknowledge this fact and move on.

AND THE ANSWER IS . . .

Now let's go back to our original question. Is it possible for one company to take fifteen months to build a warehouse when another company did it in three months? The answer: Absolutely! The question however, is: *What exactly is being built and what structures are needed to build it?*

Let's look, for example, at that small actuarial data warehouse being shown to potential customers. The data was dumped from a database, and a front end was created with a GUI development tool. No redesign was done to optimize the design for decision support processing. One reason it works so well is that the database only has a few thousand records, so response time is fast. If it was several million records, the design of the database would break down fairly quickly because it is designed for on-line transaction processing, not decision support processing. Additionally, the time it takes for data analysis, understanding decision support requirements, cleaning up data, or working with a data transformation tools was not necessary. Is this a decision support system? It is definitely being used for making decisions. From an architectural perspective, is this a data warehouse? No, because the database is actually designed for transactional processing (third normal form) and not for decision support processing.

The data warehouse architecture within your company may be implemented in a simple way using technologies that are already familiar to the development team. Or the architecture may require new platforms, new databases, transformation tools, or a variety of other new technologies and skill sets. The data warehouse is often a company's first foray into the client-server environment. If this is so within your company, the learning curve may be part of the overall time it takes to build the data warehouse. It is the implementation of the architecture and infrastructures that often increases the length of time it will take to develop a data warehouse.

Is it possible that one company took only three months while another company took fifteen months to do development? Absolutely. Unless you understand the experience levels and skill sets of the developers, and the architecture and infrastructures that were implemented, the development timelines are not valid comparisons. The questions is, once again, *what is being built and what structures must be implemented to build it?* If building a data warehouse means the design, development, and load of the database, this is achievable in three months. If building a data warehouse includes the full lifecycle implementation—from the source systems through your users doing successful decision support processing at their desktop—then three months is probably not possible.

I cannot emphasize enough how important it is to take the time to understand your architecture and infrastructures before building your data warehouse. If your architecture is set up to seamlessly handle decision support processing, then it is true that the development of these systems can go very fast. However, as a project manager who is responsible for the project plan, timelines, and budget for development of the data warehouse, wouldn't you prefer to know if you are responsible for setting up the full architecture and infrastructures for implementing the data warehouse or just the design and development of the database itself? Obviously this will have considerable effect on all aspects of the development project, including resources, timelines, tasks, deliverables, and training needs.

SUMMARY

In this chapter, you should have learned the following:

- An architecture is a set of rules or structures providing a framework for the overall design of a system or product.

- A data architecture provides a framework by identifying how data will move throughout the system and be utilized within the corporation.

- The data architecture for a data warehouse has the following distinguishing characteristics:
  - Data is extracted from source systems, databases, and files.
  - The data from the source sytems is integrated and transformed before being loaded into the data warehouse.
  - The data warehouse is a separate, read-only database designed specifically for decision support processing.

- Users access the data warehouse via some front end tool or application.

- Source fields for a data warehouse may come from different databases, different platforms, and in a variety of data types and formats.

- One database design can not efficiently provide both operational and decision support functionality.

- The generic data warehouse architecture, as well as many variations, are currently being implemented within companies.

- There is no right way to implement a data warehouse, however the basic constructs of the data warehouse architecture must be in place.

- Technical infrastructures are the technologies, platforms, databases, gateways and other components necessary to support the chosen data warehouse architecture.

- Part of building a data warehouse is finding the correct technical solutions to your decision support needs and creating a solid data warehouse architecture within the parameters you have to work with.

- One data warehouse architecture can be implemented in several ways by using different infrastructures.

- Technical training is an important technical infrastructure.

- Identifying data warehouse architecture and infrastructures should be a separate project from the actual development of your data warehouse.

Chapter 4

The Decision Support Life Cycle

LIFE CYCLES FOR SYSTEM DEVELOPMENT

The System Development Life Cycle (SDLC) for on-line transaction processing systems will usually go through several phases: Planning, Analysis, Design, Development, Testing, and Implementation. The development of client-server and distributed systems has modified the traditional SDLC, but also moves through a predictable set of tasks and deliverables from the beginning of the life cycle to the implementation of a fully functioning production system.

As would be expected, the development of a data warehouse for decision support also goes through several predictable phases, often simply called the Decision Support Life Cycle or DSLC. The Decision Support Life Cycle, while it may contain many of the same phases, is different from the traditional System Development Life Cycle. The differences in these two approaches to development emerge because the goals and the data structures of on-line transaction based systems and decision support systems are different.

ISSUES AFFECTING THE DECISION SUPPORT LIFE CYCLE

The focus of a data warehouse is data, not business processing and its associated functionality. Operational business process functionality is not a major component of the Decision Support Life Cycle. This lack of business functionality equates to a much faster development life cycle, as process modeling and other tasks associated with developing business functionality are generally not needed.

Database sizes for decision support systems can be extremely large (terabytes) with single tables potentially holding gigabytes of data. Extremely large database size has a substantial effect on the focus of the development and when in the life cycle certain tasks are done. For instance, capacity planning estimates are done as early as possible in the Decision Support Life Cycle, and Database Administration and Operations are brought into the life cycle earlier than would be customary in an on-line transaction system.

A data warehouse for decision support is often taking data from various platforms, databases, and files as source data. The use of advanced tools and specialized technologies may be necessary in the development of decision support systems, which affects tasks, deliverables, training, and project timelines.

THE DECISION SUPPORT LIFE CYCLE IN AN ARCHITECTED ENVIRONMENT

This book is focusing primarily on building a data warehouse in an architected environment. It has made a case for establishing the technical infrastructures—which are defined as the training, tools, and technologies needed for the successful development of a data warehouse and identifying the data warehouse data architecture before beginning the development of the data warehouse.

Data processing environments in which data warehouses are created vary widely. It is entirely possible to build a data warehouse without the use of data transformation technologies, with minimal technical infrastructures, and in an extremely fast timeframe. An environment where source data is homogeneous and easy to locate and extract, where only simple data transformations are needed, and where front end data access is available and usable may be a good candidate for a much faster, less architected development approach.

However, many corporations have extremely sophisticated data-processing environments, and must be able to technically integrate a variety of information sources, platforms, technologies, data structures, and databases to provide decision support information to users having a wide range of data access requirements and capabilities. These companies will find an architected approach required for the successful development of a data warehouse. Unfortunately, many companies have tried building a data warehouse without establishing the correct architectures and infrastructures, hence have not been successful with their efforts.

The Decision Support Life Cycle described below covers the full life cycle development of a data warehouse in an architected environment. The Decision Support Life Cycle is targeted to heterogeneous, sophisticated environments requiring practical and realistic guidelines for data warehouse development.

THE PHASES OF THE DECISION SUPPORT LIFE CYCLE (DSLC)

The Phases of the Decision Support Life Cycle (DSLC) are:

1. Planning
2. Gathering Data Requirements and Modeling
3. Physical Database Design and Development
4. Data Mapping and Transformation
5. Data Extraction and Load
6. Automating the Data Management Process
7. Application Development—Creating the Starter Set of Reports
8. Data Validation and Testing
9. Training
10. Rollout

The phases of the DSLC and the central points of focus for each phase will be explained.

Phase 1: Planning

Planning for a data warehouse encompasses many of the same tasks as any other type of system development project. Creating a project plan and defining realistic time estimates may be difficult for the novice (or even the experienced!) project manager, in part because there are altogether new tasks within the DSLC. It may be helpful to review the remainder of this chapter in detail before creating the project plan.

It is imperative that the data warehouse data architecture and technical infrastructures have been thought through *before* the project development begins. If the data architecture and technical infrastructures have not been established, all of the architecture and infrastructure analysis will need to be added to your project plan as tasks with the appropriate deliverables, adding substantial time and complexity to your overall project plan.

Planning for a data warehouse, as shown in Figure 4–1, is concerned with:

- Defining the project scope.
- Creating the project plan.
- Defining the necessary resources, both internal and external.
- Defining the tasks and deliverables.
- Defining timelines.
- Defining the final project deliverables.

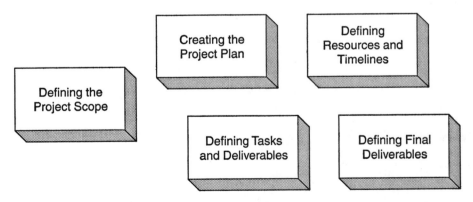

FIGURE 4–1.   Phase 1 of the Decision Support Life Cycle: Project Planning.

In addition, there are technical considerations for full life cycle development of a data warehouse that may not have been part of the technical infrastructures but will be part of the development life cycle. These technical considerations will need to be included in the project plan, with appropriate tasks and deliverables, as they require technical resources and time. These may include:

- Capacity planning (as early in the life cycle as possible).
- Archiving strategies.
- Procedures for end user access to archived data.
- Data refresh/update strategies.
- Operations and job scheduling strategies.

If the following technical infrastructures are not in place, they too will need to be part of your project plan:

- LAN/WAN
- Database connectivity
- Database gateways
- DBMS load utilities
- Configured workstations

Phase 2: Gathering Data Requirements and Modeling

This phase of the life cycle is concerned with understanding the business needs and data requirements of the users of the system. It also includes modeling these requirements. The entire requirements phase can be accomplished in as little as four to six weeks, but should not take more than ten weeks. If the process takes longer, you have too broad a scope to accomplish in a single pass. Break the project into separate phases.

Gathering Data Requirements. Gathering data requirements includes understanding:

- How the user does business.
- How the user's performance is measured.
- What attributes does the user need?
- What are the business hierarchies?
- What data do users use now and what would they like to have?
- What levels of detail or summary do the users need?

Tasks, deliverables, and schedules should be defined that will assist analysts in moving through this phase quickly. See Chapter 6 for detailed information on interviewing users and gathering requirements.

The process of building a data warehouse is iterative in nature. Once the first round of data is loaded into the data warehouse and users have a chance to see what data is available to them, there will be changes and additions requested. This is to be expected and is a normal part of the Decision Support Life Cycle. This phase of the lifecycle is purposely kept short because of the importance of the iterative process, which is an effective means of fine tuning data needs.

Information collected during this requirements gathering will directly feed the data modeling.

Data Modeling. The central focus of this task in the life cycle is to provide:

- A logical data model covering the scope of the development project including relationships, cardinality, attributes, and candidate keys.

—or—

- A Dimensional Business Model that diagrams the facts, dimensions, hierarchies, relationships and candidate keys for the scope of the development project.

For a discussion of data modeling and the scope of your modeling efforts, please see Chapter 6. In addition, the follow-

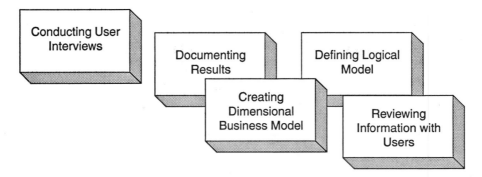

FIGURE 4–2.   Phase 2 of the Decision Support Life Cycle: Gathering Data Requirements and Modeling the Data.

ing issues can affect the timing of the data warehouse development and should be addressed before development begins if they were not resolved as technical infrastructures:

- How will derived data be reflected in your model?

- Are there clear procedures within the corporation with respect to logical models? Do you have a choice to build a logical data model or Dimensional Business Model, or must you create an ERD (entity relationship diagram)?

- If you are using a CASE tool, will the tool allow the transformation of a denormalized logical model to the physical mode for DDL generation?

- Are there procedures in place within the data modeling group so that datatypes and other modeling objects are shared among data warehouse projects?

Phase 3: Physical Database Design and Development

This phase of the DSLC covers database design and denormalization. It also has tasks critical to decision support processing and development. For the Database Design phase of the life cycle, as detailed in Figure 4–3, the focus will be on:

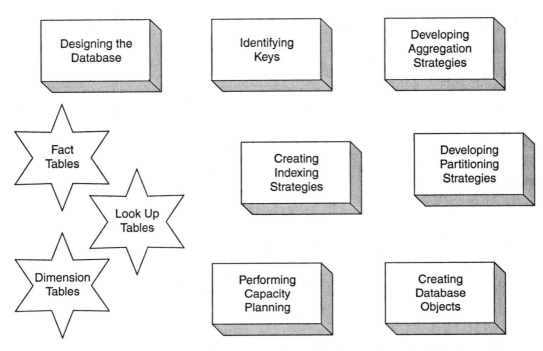

FIGURE 4–3.   Phase 3 of the Decision Support Life Cycle: Physical Database Design and Development.

- Designing the database, including fact tables, relationship tables, and description (lookup) tables.
- Denormalizing the data.
- Identifying keys.
- Creating indexing strategies.
- Creating appropriate database objects.

For this phase, it is imperative that you get training and have an understanding of:

- Decision support concepts.
- The concepts of hierarchies, dimensions, and facts.
- Star schemas.

Chapter 7, Designing the Database for a Data Warehouse, has extensive and detailed information that will assist you with this process.

At this stage you should also:

- Develop aggregation strategies.
- Develop partitioning strategies.
- Develop capacity planning estimates.

Phase 4: Data Mapping and Transformation

This is a phase that is started in conjunction with the database design phase. This phase, shown in Figure 4–4, is quite sophisticated and encompasses locating the source of the data in the operational systems, doing analysis to understand what types

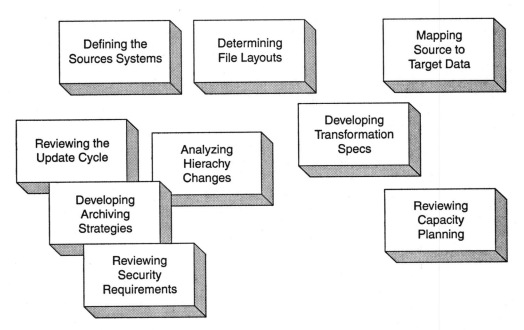

FIGURE 4–4.   Phase 4 of the Decision Support Life Cycle: Data Mapping and Transformation.

of data transformations may be needed, and mapping the source data to target data warehouse database design. This investigation is crucial to determine what data is captured. During this phase you will:

- Defining the source systems.
- Determining file layouts.
- Developing written transformation specifications for sophisticated transformations.
- Mapping source to target data.
- Reviewing capacity plans.

For each source you should determine:

- Is there end-of-year processing (summarizations) or table roll-off requirements?
- What are the archiving requirements?
- Is there any special security requirements?
- What is the update cycle?
- How often does the hierarchy change?

Phase 5: Populating the Data Warehouse

The full process of extracting, transforming, and loading data into the target database will often be done with the assistance of data transformation technology. Using a data transformation tool will affect the timing of the life cycle phases and may consolidate tasks and deliverables. The focus of this phase, illustrated in Figure 4–5, is:

- Developing procedures to extract and move the data.
- Developing procedures to load the data into the warehouse.
- Developing programs or use data transformation tools to transform and integrate data.
- Testing extract, transformation and load procedures.

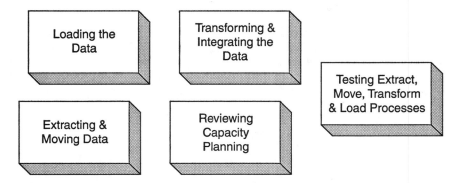

FIGURE 4–5.   Phase 5 of the Decision Support Life Cycle: Populating the Data Warehouse.

—— Tips from the Trenches 4.1 ——

AVAILABILITY OF DATA

During the first iteration of the DSLC, there may be data that is requested that for some reason cannot be delivered. This is not an unusual situation, especially for proof of concept pilot projects. For instance, if a pilot is being developed very quickly, the data structures of the requested data may be too difficult to access or the data transformations too complicated to handle in a short timeframe. Similarly, sources for requested data simply may not exist in the current systems.

It is important to know if the data is or is not available very early in the life cycle so that adjustments to the database design can be made.

A good programmer/analyst with a working knowledge of the system data is invaluable in this process and should be a part of the data warehouse development team from its inception. He or she will often know quite quickly what data is not available, and may be able to recommend and locate data alternatives to the requested decision support data.

Technical infrastructures should be in place to assist with these middle phases of data mapping, transformation, extracting and loading. These infrastructures may include:

- DBA expertise
- Data transformation tool training/expertise
- Update/refresh strategies
- Load strategies
- Operations/job scheduling
- Quality assurance procedures
- Capacity planning expertise

Phase 6: Automating Data Management Procedures

This phase is concerned with automating the extraction, transformation, and load of the data warehouse. This phase, as shown in Figure 4–6, will include:

- Automating and scheduling the data extraction process.
- Automating and scheduling the data transformation process.

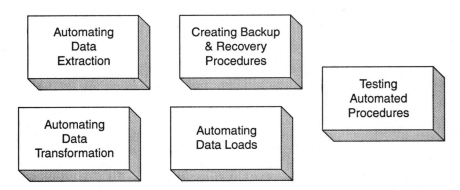

FIGURE 4–6.   Phase 6 of the Decision Support Life Cycle: Automating Data Management Procedures.

- Automating and scheduling the data load process.
- Creating backup and recovery procedures.
- Conducting a full test of all of the automated procedures.

Phase 7: Application Development— Creating the Starter Set of Reports

Application development can begin as soon as you have loaded a test subset of data. DSS application development is generally done through the use of data access tools to prebuild several reports. DSS application development and data access tools are discussed at length in Chapter 8. Figure 4–7 shows the major tasks in this phase.

Structured navigation paths to access predefined reports or data directly also must be developed. This may be as complex as writing Visual Basic code or as simple as configuring the interface of a tool. This phase also drives data validation and performance tuning. Actual development may only require several weeks of effort. However, you should plan for a larger number of elapsed weeks in your project schedule to account for the time required to correct data-related issues.

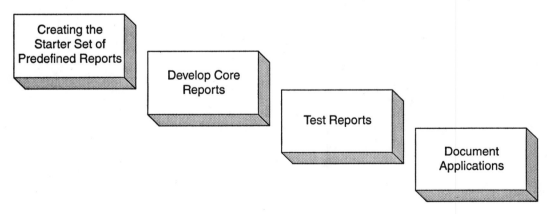

FIGURE 4–7.   Phase 7 of the Decision Support Life Cycle: Application Development— Creating the Starter Set of Reports.

This phase is concerned with :

- Creating the starter set of predefined reports.
- Developing core reports.
- Testing reports.
- Documenting applications.
- Developing navigation paths.

Phase 8: Data Validation and Testing

You should include standard data validation processes throughout the data extract, transformation, and load development phases. Basic checks on record counts—and other traditional development concepts—apply for the data warehouse also. In addition, once the data access front end has been put in place, additional validation can occur.

Phases 7 and 8, are the catalysts for iterative changes within the Decision Support Life Cycle as users work with the front end tools to interact with the data. Development will move back up the Decision Support Life Cycle to the analysis phase, working itself back down as the database modifications are made. These new data modifications will be located, extracted, mapped, transformed, and loaded into the data warehouse. Figure 4–8 illustrates the primary elements of this phase.

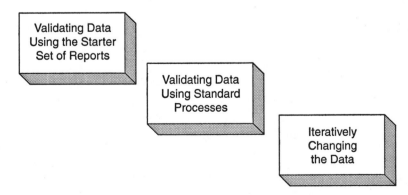

FIGURE 4–8.   Phase 8 of the Decision Support Life Cycle: Data Validation and Testing.

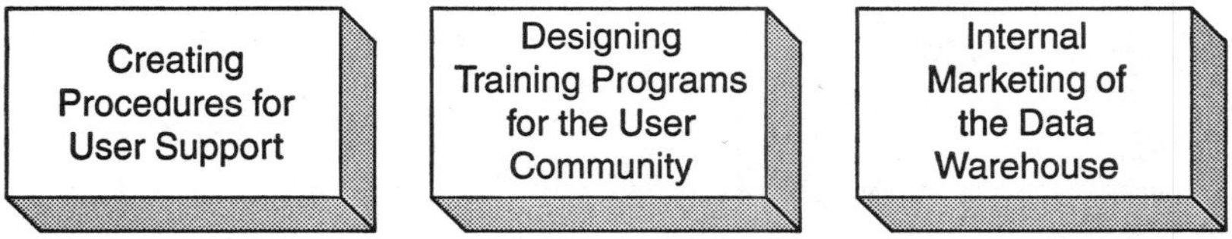

| Creating Procedures for User Support | Designing Training Programs for the User Community | Internal Marketing of the Data Warehouse |

FIGURE 4–9.   Phase 9 of the Decision Support Life Cycle: Training and User Support.

Phase 9: Training

The training phase of the Decision Support Life Cycle, as shown in Figure 4–9, is focused on creating training programs for the user community. A one-day training course on the front end tool is *not* enough. To gain real business value from your warehouse development, users of all levels will need to be trained in:

- The scope of the data in the warehouse.
- The front end access tool and how it works.
- The DSS application or starter set of reports—the capabilities and navigation paths.
- Ongoing training/user assistance as the system evolves.

See Chapter 9 for a discussion of training and support for your data warehouse.

Phase 10: Rollout

This phase of the life cycle includes the necessary tasks for the deployment of your data warehouse to the user community. These may include:

- Installing the physical infrastructures for all users. The components that must be in place are LAN/WAN, database connectivity, configured workstations and data access tool software.

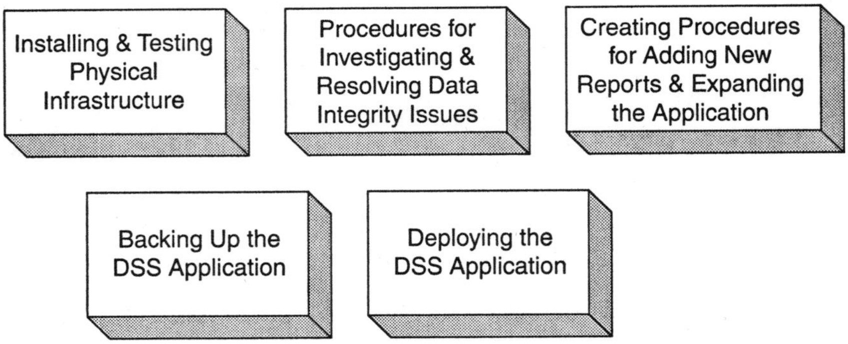

FIGURE 4–10.   Phase 10 of the Decision Support Life Cycle: Data Warehouse Rollout.

■ Deploying the DSS application.

■ Creating user support structures.

■ Creating procedures for adding new reports and expanding the DSS application.

■ Setting up procedures to backup the DSS application, not just the data warehouse.

■ Creating procedures for investigating and resolving data integrity related issues.

SUMMARY

In this chapter, you should have learned the following:

■ The lack of traditional business functionality inherent in decision support systems equates to a much faster development life cycle, as process modeling and other tasks associated with developing business functionality are not generally needed.

■ The evaluation, acquisition, and use of advanced tools and specialized technologies may be necessary in the development of decision support systems, which affects tasks, deliverables, training, and timelines within the Decision Support Life Cycle.

The different phases of the Decision Support Life Cycle:

- Planning
- Gathering Data Requirements and Modeling
- Physical Database Design & Development
- Data Mapping & Transformation
- Data Extraction & Load
- Automating the Data Management Process
- Application Development—Creating the Starter Set of Reports
- Data Validation and Testing
- Rollout and End User Support

Chapter 5

Getting Started with Data Warehouse Development

THE PROOF IS IN THE PILOT

Before creating a full-blown data warehouse, many companies first do a pilot project to get their feet wet, gain experience, show users the value of decision support information, or perhaps do a proof of concept for higher management or for a steering committee. It is amazing how many of these pilot projects are not successful or take altogether too long before deliverables are in front of the users.

If you want a successful data warehouse pilot project, a few basics should be handled from the very beginning. These are:

■ Clarify the purpose of the pilot project. What is the goal?
■ Treat the pilot as a development project—allocate appropriate resources and a project manager.

Clarify the Purpose and Goal of the Pilot Project

Why are you doing a pilot project? If the answer is: To see if a decision support system will provide a competitive edge for the corporation, an automatic bell should go off in your head. This is not a good reason to do a pilot project—it is much too broad and will be difficult to achieve.

What is the goal of the data warehouse pilot project? The answer to this question will determine how to proceed successfully with the development of your pilot. If you are doing a "proof of concept" pilot, the goal may be to show users how a system can provide useful, decision support information. In other words, proving that the concept of a data warehouse for decision support is viable and valuable to the company, and can assist them in their decision making.

One way to prove that a data warehouse for decision support will assist users in decision making is to get the data in front of the users in a way that is easily accessible, within a relatively short timeframe. The primary focus, then, would be to develop a good, accessible database design and put time and attention into assisting users in understanding the navigation and capabilities of the decision support data. This may include providing short decision support training classes, finding front end data access software users are comfortable with and work well with, and working with them to create predefined queries.

The focus of the proof of concept pilot will be on the data and the users' interaction with the decision support information. Understanding how this information will assist them in decision making will prove that the concept of a data warehouse is viable and valuable to the corporation. This can often be accomplished with a small subset of data.

The proof of concept pilot is completely different from an architecture and infrastructure pilot. An architecture and infrastructure pilot is developed to figure out how all of the components of a data warehouse work together and to understand and gain experience with the phases of the Decision Support Life Cycle. Such a pilot would develop a very small decision support database, but with data flowing through the entire data warehouse architecture. The communications, gateways, middleware tools, refresh/update strategies, and front end software—all of the technologies required to bring data from the source systems into a decision support data warehouse for easy access by a user—would be used and tested.

The main goals of this type of pilot are:

- Understanding the complexities involved in developing a data warehouse for decision support.
- Gaining experience with new tools and technologies.
- Getting a sense of realistic timelines and learning curves for tasks.
- A data warehouse providing decision support information to users.

A proof of concept data warehouse pilot project can usually be done in a much shorter timeframe than an architecture and infrastructure pilot, because all of the technical components may not need to be in place. Technologies that are familiar to the developers, programmers, and DBAs may be used in a proof of concept pilot. However, the architecture and infrastructure pilot, while taking longer, will provide a stronger knowledge base so that future projects will go more smoothly and quickly.

Treat the Pilot like a Development Project

Building a data warehouse for decision support is very often thought of as "no big deal"—simply a matter of dropping some data into a database and using a query tool on it. You might hear how finance or purchasing, for instance, is "throwing together" a decision support system because they are tired of waiting for reports.

The idea of finding a way to access information more easily is not new. Programmers have been providing reports by creating extract files off of different systems and applications for years. Doing a database dump or using one of the multiple extract files within the company and putting a front end query tool on it is not the type of data warehouse pilot being recommended here. In fact, this type of approach creates more problems than it solves, and wreaks havoc on your data warehouse data architecture. Both types of pilots, either a proof of concept pilot or architecture and infrastructure pilot (and probably any other kind), require an understanding of decision support concepts and a sound database design.

Approach a data warehouse pilot project like what it is—a development project. It should be funded, have a project manager who understands the steps within the Decision Support Life Cycle, and have the associated tasks and deliverables that will keep the pilot moving well. A successful data warehouse pilot project requires this.

Building on the Pilot

The data warehouse pilot project is rarely a throwaway. You can refine the pilot then move on to the next subject area. Usually the next subject area of the warehouse is built upon the first, or the iterative process builds upon the existing database. Since pilot projects are quite often used as the basis of ongoing data warehouse development projects, designing the database with an eye toward the future is a very good idea.

The base data should be designed well so that moving from a proof of concept pilot to a more fully developed data warehouse, for instance, may not require a full redesign of the database. The development cycle in such a situation would then be centered more on considering requirements and modification for full volumes, finding technical solutions, and creating strategies for making all the architectural components work together.

Since the database for the pilot project has an extremely high chance of being built upon, you must take the time to design the data well.

The database design of a data warehouse for decision support will be discussed in detail in Chapter 7.

With respect to pilot projects you should also be aware that several vendors in the marketplace are providing an abbreviated proof of concept. These projects, which typically last between 2 and 4 weeks, provide a visual idea of the possibilities and the benefits of a data warehouse in your environment. A subset of your data is generally loaded into a database and sample applications may be developed. You will gain the most from this type of project if you assign one or more of your data warehouse project team members to work with the vendor. This type of effort will produce for you:

- A first cut of a Dimensional Business Model.
- Ideas on how to design your physical database.
- An understanding of the cleanliness of your data.
- A working prototype of a data warehouse.
- Concrete analytical examples to serve as thought starters for your end users.
- An understanding of how your data access tool works.

Keep in mind that vendor supplied abbreviated pilots also bear several risks, including:

■ A misconception that you can really build a data warehouse in two to four weeks.

■ Not understanding the complete infrastructure required to support a production data warehouse.

■ Large data volumes are significantly different than small prototype volumes, both in database design and data administration.

■ The full life cycle is not considered; many shortcuts are made due to time constraints.

■ You may end up with only a partial understanding of full life cycle data warehouse development—just enough to be dangerous, but not enough to be effective.

Beware of any abbreviated proof of concept project that takes more than a few weeks. It may really be a pilot project and should be handled as previously discussed in this chapter.

CHOOSING A BUSINESS AREA FOR DATA WAREHOUSE DEVELOPMENT

If you are committed to building a data warehouse for decision support, and have not yet made a decision on the business area, consider first what drives the revenues for your company. This will usually be a primary consideration in developing a data warehouse. Then consider:

■ Sales analysis
■ Finance
■ Marketing
■ Market segmentation
■ Customer profiles

Although many areas within the company can benefit from decision support information, these areas lend themselves well to decision support processing. Finance, sales analysis, marketing, customer profiling, and market segmentation are especially beneficial areas for development as companies seek to become more competitive.

Finance may be a good candidate for your first data warehouse. Programmers have been trying to do good analytical processing on financial data for years using traditional programming techniques. For good reason. It is important to understand what can influence the finances of a corporation. Finance also lends itself well to decision support processing because the amount of data is usually finite, and the scope of the project limited. Also, financial information is often held in homogeneous systems within corporations, as suites of financial software from the same vendor and running on the same platform are often purchased and used together. The finite data, limited scope, and homogeneity make financial systems a good choice for data warehouse development.

Sales or marketing analysis are also good candidates for your first warehouse. These areas are quite data reliant—analysts are looking at the numbers to make business decisions on a daily basis already. Providing good quality, multidimensional data that can be manipulated across many dimensions would be using data as a corporate resource. These areas drive the revenue for the organization and are keys to business success.

Market segmentation and customer profiling—understanding what products are being sold, where they are selling, what is affecting their sales, and who they are being sold to—is fundamental to business profitability and success.

This type of fundamental information, within most corporations, is incomplete or nonsense, and getting to it is difficult. It is also of incredible value to decision makers.

Using historical data to build strong customer profiles and creating targeted marketing strategies from these profiles is one key to keeping a corporation competitive. For this reason, marketing and its associated specialties, such as customer pro-

---

—— *Tips from the Trenches 5.1* ——

CHOOSING A BUSINESS AREA

1. Do simple in-house marketing on decision support technologies so business areas within the company have an idea what a decision support system can offer.

2. Clarify the goal of the development. One business area may be a better choice than another for fulfilling this goal.

3. Have a high level sponsor. It is imperative for the success of this type of development.

4. Work with a business area or department that is excited about the project and getting access to decision support information. A positive attitude and a high level of cooperation go a long way toward success in developing systems.

5. Finance, sales management, brand analysis, marketing or market segmentation are good candidate business areas for your first development project.

6. Keep the first project small, much smaller in scope than you originally assumed.

---

filing and market segmentation, are good candidates for data warehouse development, but may be a bit more difficult to implement on your first project.

ENSURING A SUCCESSFUL DATA WAREHOUSE

Now that you have chosen a subject area for your pilot project, you are ready to get started! In our experience, we have found the following eight points, "The Big Eight," are critical to ensure a successful data warehouse development project.

—— Tips from the Trenches 5.2 ——

BUILDING A SUCCESSFUL DATA WAREHOUSE
"THE BIG EIGHT"

1. Be clear on the goal of the data warehouse.

2. Understand the chosen data warehouse data architecture.

3. Make sure the technical infrastructures are in place.

4. Clarify the project team's responsibilities and the final project deliverable.

5. Understand the difference between operational and decision support information.

6. Get the correct training.

7. Get the right resources.

8. Choose front end data access software based on users' needs and abilities.

Be Clear on Your Goal

One of the first questions to clarify in any type of data warehouse development is simple: Why are you building one? Your goal for developing a data warehouse will have a broad-range affect on what gets developed, what data goes into the data warehouse, and your parameters for success. A data warehouse goal statement should be specific and written. The goal will have a considerable affect on the scope of the project and will provide boundaries so that the scope isn't continually changing and expanding.

Understand the Chosen Data Warehouse Architecture

A diagram of your data warehouse architecture should be on the desk of every member of the development team. This is the high-level blueprint that will be used to develop the decision support system. The choice of data architecture and infrastructures will determine many aspects of how the system is developed, such as types of database design and granularity levels, options for update/refresh technologies, training, and timing within the development life cycle. The architecture and infrastructure also provide a solid basis for explaining decision support system development within the corporation.

Make Sure the Technical Infrastructures Are in Place or Being Put in Place

The technical infrastructures—the tools, platforms, databases, communications, training, and so on—usually require a bit of time to put into place. New hardware and software may need to be purchased and installed; data transformation tools must be reviewed and chosen; and networks, gateways and communications must be set up. These technologies take time to purchase, install, learn, and fine tune. Technical infrastructures should be determined and in the process of installation before the warehouse development begins.

Clarify the Project Team's Responsibility and Final Deliverable

Building a data warehouse for decision support in an architected environment brings together many departments, technologies, and skills. It is also common for the Information Technology Department to team up with a business area to co-sponsor and co-fund a data warehouse project. Especially in situations where development is crossing departmental boundaries, it is a good idea to clarify the responsibilities of everyone involved in the development. Each team member must be responsible for his or her part in development. For instance, clarify responsibility for:

- ■ Modeling data requirements
- ■ Database design
- ■ Interfacing with business users and gathering data requirements
- ■ Choosing, learning, and using the data transformation tool
- ■ Front end software selection, purchase, and training
- ■ Finding the best source of data
- ■ Setting up and testing networks, gateways, and databases
- ■ Buying and installing hardware and software
- ■ Establishing security
- ■ Defining update/refresh strategies
- ■ User support and training

All companies set up their development teams differently. Some companies create a team that encompasses all of the necessary skills. Other companies have their own corporate infrastructures well developed, making it immediately evident what department or person would be responsible for specific tasks. Other companies are quite disorganized in their development and would benefit greatly by clarifying what group, department, or person is responsible for the different tasks that make up the full life cycle development of a data warehouse for decision support. Clarifying responsibilities and what the final deliverable will be is an especially important aspect of a successful project.

Make Sure the Members of the Project Team and the Users Understand the Difference between Operational and Decision Support Data

Operational data is used to run the day-to-day operations of the business, while decision support data supports analytical processing used for decision making and strategic planning. Decision support data is usually historical in nature, since monitoring trends, gauging profitability, or understanding what products are being bought are analytical processing that requires an understanding of how the data is changing over time. The definition of decision support data and how you will be using such data in your company, should be used as the basis of gathering data requirements and doing database design. Whenever there is confusion about data content, especially required levels of detail, always go back to the definitions of decision support data and analytical processing.

Get the Correct Training

It is extremely important that the project team members have a good understanding of decision support technologies. They should understand the difference between transaction processing and analytical processing systems and understand the phases in the Decision Support Life Cycle. Team members should also understand why the database design for decision support systems is different from on-line transaction systems, and how that design is different. Get the training needed to provide a solid base of decision support knowledge to all the team members before the project starts. Find a class in building a data warehouse and actively seek out decision support articles, books, and knowledgeable people. Get vendor training in the data transformation tool of choice and set aside some time in the project plan for practicing with the tool. Choices in front end data access software are extremely varied in sophistication and functionality. Certain members of the team should be well trained in whatever software is chosen. It is quite difficult to expound on the wonders of all the fantastic decision support data if the front end is more sophisticated than you are!

Get the Right Resources

Many companies may not have development teams with expertise in decision support processing and development. Like any new development, finding someone who has done it before and whose knowledge you can leverage will speed up your development. A very experienced project manager who has never implemented a data warehouse will not know all that is neccessary for a project. Don't expect him or her to. Provide someone to guide and coach that person—he or she will quickly learn the ropes. If you do not have decision support development expertise within your corporation, be encouraged to find a consultant with this expertise. Developers who have had experience working through the development cycle and in finding technical solutions to the thornier issues in data warehouse development are extremely valuable. The amount of time the company will save with a consultant who is experienced in data warehouse development, data warehouse data architecture, and/or data transformation technologies is substantial.

Additionally, find other companies that have successfully implemented and are using their warehouses. These companies can provide valuable information on what worked for them, where they hit development snags, how they incorporated database change procedures, how they marketed and rolled out the data warehouse, information on products and vendors that work, as well as a multitude of other information that only experience can provide.

For your data warehouse development project, resources or skills that you will need include:

- Someone with experience building data warehouses to assist you in creating the project plan.
- Architecture and infrastructure planning experience.
- Business or data analysts who know the data well—where it is, how it is used, and how to access it.
- Access to different levels of personnel who understand the kinds of decision support questions being asked and who know the business well.

■ A well versed DBA and star schema database design expertise.

■ A hands-on project manager, preferably one with decision support experience and a technical background.

■ Team members with a good understanding of the business, the data, and how it is used are imperative to a successful data warehouse project.

In addition you will need access to the personnel who handle networking, communications, workstation and software installation, capacity planning, operations, and training.

Choose Front End Data Access Software Based on User Needs and Abilities

Many of the query tools on the market are extremely sophisticated and are directed toward application development. They require a good knowledge of relational databases in addition to the underlying data structures and are not readily learned by business users. The choice of query tools can significantly affect how well the data warehouse is received in the user community, how eager or reluctant (due to perceived or real learning curve) users will be in using the warehouse, and how positively the corporate grapevine will influence the acceptance and use of the warehouse.

Making data truly accessible is a significant aspect of warehouse development. It is often misunderstood or overlooked. A realistic appraisal of user's needs, abilities, and comfort level with front end technology and then use of the appropriate front end software is an absolute requirement for a successful data warehouse for decision support. An entire chapter, Chapter 8, has been devoted to making timely data, accessible and should provide you with substative assistance in this critical area of data warehouse development.

SUMMARY

In this chapter, you should have learned the following:

- ■ The data warehouse pilot should be approached like any other development project, with the appropriate funding, resources, and a project manager who understands the Decision Support Life Cycle.

- ■ The primary focus of a proof of concept pilot will be on the front end and the user's interaction with the decision support information. This type of pilot can often be accomplished with a small subset of data.

- ■ An architecture and infrastructure pilot is developed to gain experience in the technicalities of how all of the components of the data warehouse architecture work together. Additionally, you will gain experience with the full Decision Support Life Cycle.

- ■ The database for the pilot project has a high chance of being built upon, so the database, even for a small project, must be designed well.

- ■ Abbreviated proof of concept pilots, taking only a few weeks, are being offered by vendors to provide a visual idea of the possibilities and benefits of the data warehouse. Be clear on the benefits and risks of such pilots, so that you can use them to your best advantage.

- ■ Clarify the goal of your pilot project development; one business area may be a better choice than another for fulfilling this goal, and increasing your liklelihood of success.

- ■ Always have a high level sponsor for the development of a data warehouse.

- ■ Finance, sales management, brand analysis, and marketing are good candidates for choosing a business areas for your initial development.

- ■ The "Big Eight" are fundamental aspects of building a successful data warehouse that should not be ignored.

■ The resources or skills that you will need to build a data warehouse include:

■ A cross section of users who know the business well and have a specific business problem to address.

■ A well versed DBA and database designer who understand how to design decision support databases.

■ A hands on project manager, preferably one with decision support experience and technical expertise.

■ Analysts who know the business and the data inside and out, and have well developed communication and interviewing skills.

■ Access to personnel who handle networking, communications, workstation and software installation, capacity planning, operations, and training.

■ A realistic appraisal of the users' analysis needs, abilities, and comfort level with front end technology, and the purchase of the appropriate front end software to respond to these different levels of users, is an absolute requirement for a successfully used data warehouse.

Chapter 6

Gathering Data Requirements

A PROPER MINDSET

It is important to understand that building a data warehouse is somewhat different than developing transaction systems. This is especially true when you are trying to gather requirements from the users. Typically, system development revolves around well-defined specifications. The paradox in building a data warehouse is to develop a system to support undefined requests.

Your job as a data warehouse developer is to recognize that your main focus in developing this system is to provide information to users. One ramification of this is that you have to be much more open minded when you gather data requirements because without prior decision support experience your users may not always know what their next question could be. Another part of your challenge is that many users have not had training in analytical processing and have not had experience using the advanced decision support front end tools that are currently on the market. This lack of experience means that they cannot imagine or visualize the broad range of capabilities that may be available to them.

USER INTERVIEWS

The Purpose of Interviews

The primary purpose of collecting end user requirements for a data warehouse is to understand how users conduct their business, what data they currently use, and what they would like to do in the future. This gives you, the data warehouse developer, the business perspective that must be delivered to the user population. A key point to keep in mind throughout the project is that users will always ask questions of the decision support system from their frame of reference. If you do not understand that frame of reference, you could deliver a system that may theoretically be fabulous, but end users will have trouble using it, or the performance will be incredibly poor since you have designed for a completely different set of parameters.

The main things that you need to come away from the interview process with are:

■ A broad business perspective, for example, that the company is planning to branch out into a specific business area over the next five years.

■ Specific details about the data and key elements to be included in the initial implementation of the data warehouse.

■ An understanding of the core use of the initial data.

■ An understanding the common information that may be used for another business unit or when additions are made.

■ An understanding of other users who need to access or could leverage the initial data.

To ensure success it is important to have systems analysts or data modelers participate in the interviewing process. If your staff has not been exposed to data warehouse and decision support development, it will be well worth the investment to include an experienced DSS consultant in your project team.

Setting up Successful Interviews

The most successful projects have input from key people within the end user community. These people tend to be very much in demand. You need to make sure that they understand the importance of their participation and give them plenty of advance notice to ensure their availability.

Who to Interview

To gain the complete understanding of the business it is important who you choose to interview. You will need a cross section of the following groups:

- Analysts and users from the target business functions.
- Managers from the target business functions.
- Analysts and users from related business functions.
- Managers from related business functions.
- Executives.

—— Tips from the Trenches 6.1 ——

SETTING UP SUCCESSFUL INTERVIEWS

1. Setting up the interview schedule should be one of the first things you do when starting a project.

2. Get on the user's calendars.

3. Conduct a maximum of two interviews a day. Give yourself time to review your notes between sessions.

4. Provide a framework for the users by sending out sample interview questions in advance.

5. Have your sponsor and/or appropriate managers send out a memo regarding the project, and the need for their participation.

6. Ask users to bring with them sample reports that they currently receive, or create, and ideas about what they want to have.

7. Publish the entire interview schedule—that way others can see who else is involved.

8. Make sure you leave time to capture a rough draft of each interview on paper within one day of the actual interview.

Within the cross section of the above groups, it is important that you interview the highly technical power users. You need to talk to key influencers, whether or not they are technically savvy. A brief description about the structure of the interview and goal for talking with each of the above groups follows.

Key End Users and Analysts from the Target Business Functions.

Spend time with the people who will be the primary audience for the system. The focus for this interview is to understand the day-to-day analysis—what is performed manually, what reports are created, and what types of ad hoc questions are being handled.

You should try to limit the number of people interviewed at one time to a maximum of four.

These interviews will take a minimum of two hours. They could take as long as four if the users have a great deal of information they wish to share.

The first interviews you conduct tend to take longer that subsequent interviews as terms and practices are learned. Try to be sensitive to the interpersonal dynamics of a group. Try to keep any single interview with peers, rather than with managers and employees. Some people are reluctant to speak freely if in an interview with their boss or their boss's boss.

Managers from the Target Business Functions.

Again these interviews should take two hours, with a maximum of four people. The primary goal here is to understand the business objectives. In the best world, how would your staff spend their time? What analyses do you wish you could get more frequently? What analyses do you perform yourself? What do you do with reports that are provided to you?

Analysts & Users from Related Business Functions.

Again, a two-hour interview with no more than four people should provide the information you need. The most useful people to talk to are those who interact directly with the data and/or business function that is the primary target. Keep this group focused on how they could use the same data and what related data is integrated to perform additional analysis. The focus of this interview is to understand the dependencies and shared data between the business groups.

Managers from Related Business Functions. It may prove to be useful to conduct individual interviews with this group, since they will have diverse responsibilities. These interviews could be reduced to one hour.

Executives. The executive sponsor and related executives should be interviewed individually. The interviews should be thirty minutes long, at most one hour. Even getting this much time may be a challenge for this level in the organization. Executive interviews should be done last. The executive vision will pull together all of the pieces of the puzzle that you have been collecting from the other interviews. This level of interview is critical to understanding the overall goals for the company. These users tend to have a great deal of vision of where they want their department/division to be in the immediate future and for the next three to five years.

This also is a visible sign of support to the rest of the organization of the importance of this project. Other people on the interview schedule will take the sessions more seriously when they see high level involvement.

What to Ask End Users

First of all, you will ask different questions of the executives than of the managers and analysts. So let's start with the managers and analysts.

Job Responsibilities

- Describe your position.
- How is your performance measured?
- What are the key business issues you face today?

Current Analysis.   It is important to understand the flow of information into and out of the department. In many cases the effort to simply handle incoming information, perform cursory analysis, and then create outgoing reports takes up all of many analysts' time. The ability to expedite and automate these processes will be very well received by the analysts.

What You Receive

- What reports do you currently get?
- Which ones do you use?
- How often do you receive this report?
- What do you look for? (look for what is highlighted)
- What else do you do with this?

More often than not, users start with a hard copy report, add several calculations by hand or re-key the data into a spreadsheet for further analysis. Do not feel bad if you find people doing this in your company. You will begin to appreciate the need for the data warehouse and your efforts!

What You Create

- What reports do you create?
- How often do you perform this analysis?
- Who gets this information?
- Do other groups create this same report? If so, who?
- How is it used?
- How long does it take you to create it?
- Where do you get the information?
- If you had the time, what are the next steps you would take to analyze this information?

Ad Hoc Analysis.   Most end users will not be able to define what their ad hoc requirements are. From their perspective, if they have all of the data they might ever need for the last ten years at the transaction level of detail, they will be able to perform their analyses. Since this is rather unrealistic, you must ask probing questions to understand the nature of the ad hoc questions. This will allow you to predict the type of analyses that may be required in the future.

- What kinds of ad hoc analyses do you do?
- Who asks the original question? Customer, manager . . . ?
- How do you fulfill these requests today?
- Do you have any examples of what you have done in the past?

Do not be surprised if several discussions occur along the following lines: Where did you get that report? How did you get charts instead of reports? Can I get a copy of that? I didn't know you were doing that too . . . .

Business Analyses.   If you are familiar with the business you may pose a series of specific questions that are topical. For instance:

- How do you develop promotional programs?
- How do you evaluate promotional effectiveness?
- How often do you perform vendor reviews?
- What analysis is performed to support the decision to buy?
- How do you manage your inventory levels?

Data Specific Information.   Summarize the different data sources that have been mentioned so far. Make sure that you understand:

- Where does the data come from?
- How often is it updated?
- What level of detail is included?
- Who is responsible for it?

Then explore other data sources. Make sure that you ask the same questions as above. Understand the business hierarchies within the data sources. Get up and draw on the board what you think the structures look like, or better yet, have them draw it for you. Almost every organization sells products, has an internal sales structure, and tracks performance over time.

So, for each of these general dimensions, make sure you understand the following:

■ At what level do you currently perform most of your analysis? Why? Sometimes it is where it makes sense, other times it is because that is all they have access to.

■ What is the lowest level of detail that exists in the organization?

■ Are there multiple hierarchies? For example, often there will be a rollup of stores into marketing areas and a different rollup into the internal sales structure for the company.

■ When does your fiscal year end?

■ What are the other characteristics of time? For instance, shipment information is monthly, but syndicated POS data comes in thirteen 4-week periods, and you set up your business calendar on a 4-4-5 week structure per quarter.

If you do not know where to start, look at the reports. Where are there subtotals? Grand totals? What are the primary headings of the reports? This will give you the starting point for the dimensions, as well as the hierarchies within those dimensions.

A Wish List

■ Make sure you get a wish list—What would you want to be able to do if there were no financial or time or technical constraints in your way? Golfing four days a week is not a valid answer. In many cases, their wildest imagination barely begins to touch on what you may already be planning to include as part of your data warehouse and decision support solution. Just make sure to bring them back to reality. Remember, good project management and interviewing skills includes managing end users' expectations.

■ Ask them what else they think you need to know that you have not yet asked.

As you work your way through the process, make sure that you understand the business hierarchical relationships. Almost every data warehouse will have at least a product, a geography, and a time hierarchy.

Do not promise anything in the meetings. After you have completed the entire interviewing process, priorities may change or key data elements may not be available. The goal of the interview process is to share information, not to cut deals.

What to Ask Executives

Be brief and concise with your questions, you will have very little time with this type of person. Also, don't bring in ten people to ask questions and/or to observe. Include two, or at most three people. If you have any specific questions about analysis or information this executive uses, ask who can provide you with an in depth understanding of that analysis rather than getting into the details at the moment.

Here are some questions you may want to ask:

■ What are your job responsibilities?

■ What are your corporate objectives?

■ What are the critical success factors for meeting those objectives?

■ What could prevent you from meeting those objectives?

■ What are the most pressing business problems you see today?

- What is the financial impact of solving these business problems?
- What is it that you want information about on a daily basis?
- What are your analysis requirements?
- What opportunities exist to improve profits?
- How do you compare to your competitors?

Also be prepared to discuss how the project is going. This person will probably have an interest in the progress and cooperation of his/her staff. If you have any *major* issues, be prepared to bring them up with a suggestion for what you will need to resolve the issue.

Documenting What You Heard

Writing up what you are learning in the interviews should be done as you go rather than waiting until all of the interviews have been completed. By the time you have talked to everyone, you may not be able to remember who said what—even if you keep thorough notes. Some people like to record the interviews on tape. If you choose to do this, make sure that you ask prior to doing so.

The interview summaries serve several key purposes:

- Capture the knowledge and what was said.
- Advance your understanding of the business.
- Serve as valuable documentation for the future.
- Provide documentation to educate new team members.

Always summarize what you have learned in writing. This is critical for understanding and integrating data requirements for your data warehouse. Interview documentation also serves as a valuable roadmap into the future.

Organize the information into the following sections:

- *Job Responsibilities:* Include a brief summary of what was shared.

- *Analysis:* Include a description of the different types of analyses that are currently performed. Examples are sales trend analysis, promotion analysis, price gap analysis, and claims summary. Also include a description of the types of analysis they would like to perform.

- *Data Requirements:* Include a description of each data field that was mentioned, and as much detail as you know about that field, including its source and how it is used.

- *Miscellaneous:* This section serves to capture other important concepts.

After you have completed writing the summary, share it with everyone who was interviewed. Get their input: You may be surprised at some of the misunderstandings that can occur.

After each group has approved its summary, bring it all together. This can be as simple as publishing all of the final interview summaries to writing a full analysis of the overall research.

As you take the time to document, remember that this will provide the foundation for future data warehouse and decision support development efforts. Also, if you do a good job, when you are wildly successful you can quickly transition a replacement in, so you can tackle your new job when you are promoted.

What You Have to Know for DSS

So now you have more details about the business than you ever wanted to know. How do you wade through all those details to determine how to build your data warehouse? First, let's review what you really need to know:

- Business entities and their attributes.

- Relationships between the entities, including all of the hierarchical relationships.

■ What business measures are used for analysis.

■ The base facts required to create the business measures.

■ Specific calculations used to create new facts.

■ If and how the facts can be aggregated.

DEVELOPING THE DATA MODEL

Data modeling is really the process of translating business concepts into a diagrammatic format that can be converted into actual physical data structures. Explanations of both Dimensional Business Models and Logical Data Models and their relevance to data warehouse development follow.

Dimensional Business Model

The users have a business model that drives how they perform their day-to-day business. Although they may not be experts at heuristic processing; end users usually have a fairly good idea of the metrics they care about, the dimensions they look at information by, the hierarchies within the dimensions, and how these metrics relate to each other.

The data warehouse must reflect this end-user business model. A simple way to organize all of the information you have gathered is to segregate business entities and attributes into facts and dimensions. This is called a Dimensional Business Model as shown in Figure 6–1.

A Dimensional Business Model is a set of diagrams developed in presentation software, requiring no specialized tools. It is a simple model showing metrics, dimensions, and relationships that can easily be presented back to users for their verification. When presenting to users, start with the dimensions then move into details about each individual dimension.

Within each dimension, or group, you will then define the hierarchy (Figure 6–2).

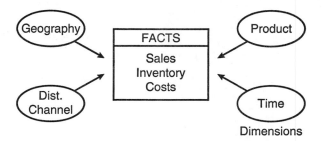

FIGURE 6–1. Example of a high level Dimensional Business Model.

The data model could also be a graphical description of the simple star schema. In that case, the logical model and the physical models will be identical with the exception of physical table partitioning. Figure 6–3 shows an example.

With any of these diagrams, you must use business labels and not internal table or column names. At this time, you can also confirm the proper business terms that will be used during the implementation of the data warehouse front end access tool.

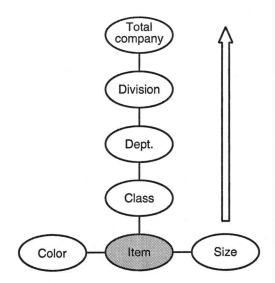

FIGURE 6–2. Example of a hierarchy within the product dimension for a retailer.

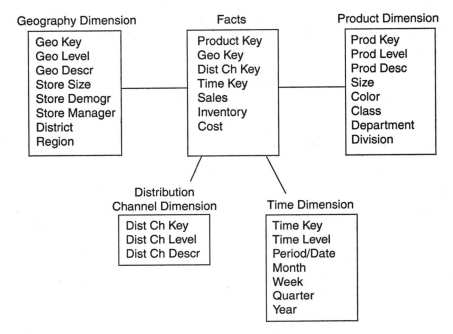

FIGURE 6–3.   Example of a star schema as a Dimensional Business Model.

Logical Data Model

Traditional logical data modeling, such as the development of entity relationship diagrams is sometimes applied to data warehouse development. The need to document a detailed logical data model is driven, to a large degree, by your corporate culture. Some organizations do not have a data modeling function, and do not have an enterprise wide data model. At the other end of the spectrum, some companies have entire groups that specialize in data modeling. This type of organization may also have in place, or is well on its way to having, a corporate data model. Your organization may require a logical data model be developed with the standard tool prior to allowing any tables to be created in any corporate database. It is important to note that a successful data warehouse does not require

---

—— Tips from the Trenches 6.2 ——

THE BASICS OF DATA MODELING

1. DO NOT use a data warehouse project to learn how to do data modeling.

2. DO NOT embark on development of the entire corporate data model under the guise of building a data warehouse.

3. Keep your model focused in the core area of development.

4. Simple structures may not warrant the effort.

5. Complex data should be modeled.

6. The model should include entities, relationships, cardinalities, attributes and candidate keys.

7. Many data modeling tools will allow you to create an appropriate logical data model, but do not support transformation to a physical star schema.

---

the development of a full and complete logical data model. In many cases, the development of a Dimensional Business Model is sufficient to drive the development of a data warehouse.

SUMMARY

In this chapter, you should have learned the following:

■ A good method of gathering requirements for a data warehouse is by conducting a series of interviews with a cross section of the user community within the scope of your project.

- The fundamentals of interviewing—who to interview, what to ask, and what the primary goal of the interview will be.

- The structure of the interview is important—limit them to a maximum of 2 per day, with a maximum of 4 users. Interviews should last only 2 to 4 hours.

- Always capture a rough draft of the information gathered at the interview within 2 hours.

- What you need to know for decision support systems is:
  - Business entities and their attributes.
  - Relationships between entities.
  - Hierarchies.
  - What facts are used.
  - What are the base facts.
  - What calculations are used to create new facts.
  - If and how the facts can be aggregated.

- The Dimensional Business Model is a simple way to segregate and diagram the facts and dimensions gathered throughout the interviewing process, and are easily understood by users. These can often be used to replace an Entity Relationship Diagram (ERD).

- If data structures are simple, a full logical data model may not be required for the development of a data warehouse—a Dimensional Business Model can be used instead. For extremely complex data, you may wish to do an ERD. Do so only for the scope of your project

- Do not use the data warehouse project to learn how to do data modeling.

- Many tools will allow you to create an appropriate logical model, but do not support transformation into a physical star schema.

Chapter 7

Designing the Database for a Data Warehouse

TRANSACTION-PROCESSING DATABASES

Transaction-processing systems are designed to capture information and to be updated very quickly; they are constantly changing and are often on-line 24 hours a day. Examples of transaction-processing systems include order entry, scanner-based point-of-sale registers, automatic teller machines, and airline reservation applications. These systems provide operational support to a business and are used to run a business.

Transaction-processing systems have the following characteristics:

- High transaction rate.
- Constantly changing: A large number of transactions produce data that is in a constant state of change.
- No redundancy: Redundant data is avoided in order to ensure data integrity.
- Predictable SQL queries: To ensure consistent response time, SQL statements are simple, predefined, and tested. Indexes are optimized for these SQL statements.
- Recoverable: To ensure against data loss, two-phase-commit and rollback mechanisms, continuous transaction logs, and mirrored disk technology are employed.

These goals are achieved by relational database schemas with a high degree of normalization that results in many tables and many joins. Normalization provides for data integrity and a complex schema that is easily manipulated by the applications using it, but difficult to understand by the people needing the data.

Much of the information in this chapter is from the "Warehouse Administrators' Guide" from Red Brick Systems, Inc. Diagrams, although modified, are also courtesy of Red Brick Systems, Inc.

DECISION SUPPORT DATABASES

Decision support systems are designed to allow analysts to extract information quickly and easily. The data being analyzed is often historical in nature: daily, weekly, and yearly results. Examples of decision support systems include applications for analysis of sales revenue, marketing information, insurance claims, and customer profiling. These systems provide the information needed for business analysis and planning, and are used to manage the business.

Decision support systems have the following characteristics:

- Understandable: Data structures must be readily understood by users, often requiring denormalization and pre-stored aggregations.
- Mostly static: Most changes to the database occur in a controlled manner when data is loaded according to a predefined schedule.
- Unpredictable and complex SQL queries: SQL query statements submitted against the database vary considerably and unpredictably from query to query. They can contain long, complex SQL SELECT statements that make comparisons or require sequential processing; these queries might reference many thousands or millions of records in a database.
- Advanced business measurements often require multiple SQL statements.
- Multiple/large/iterative result sets should be supported.
- Recoverable: Regular backups, or snapshots, of the static database ensure against data loss.

STAR SCHEMA DATABASE DESIGN

The goals of a decision support database are often achieved by a database design called a star schema. A star schema design is a simple structure with relatively few tables and well-defined join paths. This database design, in contrast to the normalized structure used for transaction-processing databases, provides fast query response time and a simple schema that is readily understood by the analysts and end users, even those who are not familiar with database structures.

The Benefits of Using a Star Schema

It is best to make the decision before beginning data modeling and physical database design to use a star schema or a more traditional relational database design. In both cases, you will optimize performance of the database by denormalizing and partitioning data. However, using a star schema provides some benefits that a regular relational structure cannot. The star schema is quickly becoming the standard for data warehouse database design because it:

- Creates a database design providing fast response times.
- Provides a design that can easily be modified or added to throughout development iterations, and as the data warehouse grows.
- Parallels, in the database design, how the end users customarily think of and use the data.
- Simplifies the understanding and navigation of metadata for both developers and end users.
- Broadens the choices of front end data access tools, as some products require a star schema design.

Understanding Star Schema Design—Facts and Dimensions

A star schema contains two types of tables, fact tables and dimension tables. Fact tables, sometimes called major tables, contain the quantitative or factual data about a business—the information being queried. This information is often numerical measurements and can consist of many columns and millions of rows. Dimension tables, sometimes called minor tables, are smaller and hold descriptive data that reflect the dimensions of a business. SQL queries then use predefined and user-defined join paths between fact and dimension tables, with constraints on the data to return selected information.

For example, a fact table in a sales database might contain the sales revenue for the company products for each customer, in each geographic market, over a period of time. The dimension tables in this database define the customers, products, geographic markets, and time periods used in the fact table.

A well-thought-out schema provides dimension tables that allow a user to browse a database to become familiar with the information in it. The user can then write constraints for queries so that only the information that satisfies those constraints is returned from the database.

VARIETIES OF STAR SCHEMAS

How to Read the Diagrams

A series of figures is used throughout the rest of this chapter to illustrate specific schema concepts. The following conventions are used throughout:

- The items listed under each table heading indicate columns in the table.
- Primary and foreign key columns are boxed.
- The primary key columns in each table are shaded; however, foreign keys that are not part of the primary key are not shaded.
- Foreign key relationships are indicated by lines connecting tables. Notice that although the primary key value must be unique in each row of a dimension table, that value can occur multiple times in the foreign key in the fact table—a

many-to-one relationship as represented by the crow's feet symbol on the connecting lines.

■ Non-key columns in a fact table are referred to as data columns; in a dimension table, as attributes.

The simplicity of the figures is intentional and used to explain concepts. An extensive and more realistic example will be diagrammed at the end of the chapter.

—— Tips from the Trenches 7.1 ——

UNDERSTANDING FACTS AND DIMENSIONS

1. Think of how an end-user or analyst looks at business performance.

   ■ A salesperson analyzes revenue by customer, product, market, and time period.

   ■ A financial analyst tracks actuals and budgets by line item, product, and time period.

   ■ A marketing person reviews shipments by product, market, and time period.

2. The facts—what is being analyzed or reviewed in each case—are revenue, actuals and budgets, and shipments: These items belong in fact tables.

3. The business dimensions—the "by" items—are product, market, time period, and line item: these items belong in dimension tables.

4. You are analyzing facts by, or through, different dimensions.

Simple Star Schemas

Each table must have a primary key, which is a column or group of columns (the key, the whole key, and nothing but the key) whose contents uniquely identify each row. In a simple star schema, the primary key for the fact table is composed of one or more foreign keys; a foreign key is a column in one table whose values are defined by the primary key in another table. When a database is created, the SQL statements used to create the tables will designate the columns that are to form the primary and foreign keys.

Study Figure 7–1 below which illustrates the relationship between fact and dimension tables. This figure has a single fact table and three dimension tables. The fact table has a primary key composed of three foreign keys, Key1, Key2, and Key3, each of which is the primary key of a dimension table.

Figure 7–2 illustrates a sales database designed as a simple star schema. In the fact table, the primary key is composed of three foreign keys, Product_Id, Period_Id, and Market_Id. Each of these foreign keys references a primary key in one of the dimension tables.

Notice the many-to-one relationships between the foreign

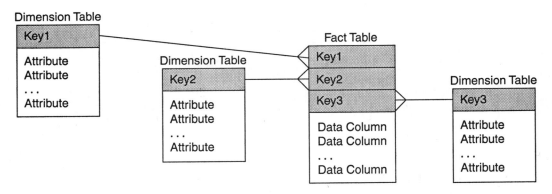

FIGURE 7–1.   The relationship of fact and dimension tables in a simple star schema.

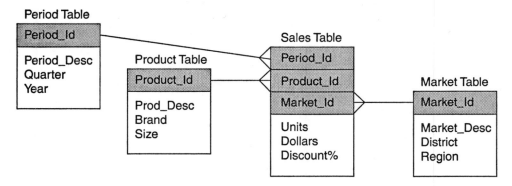

FIGURE 7–2.   A sales database with a simple star schema.

keys in the fact table and the primary keys they reference in the dimension tables. For example, the product table defines the products. Each row in the product table represents a distinct product and has a unique product identifier. That product identifier can occur multiple times in the sales table representing sales of that particular product during each period and in each market.

Multiple Fact Tables

A star schema can contain multiple fact tables. In some cases, multiple fact tables exist because they contain unrelated facts or because periodicity of the load times differs. For example, internal shipment data is available weekly, but syndicated data is only provided every four weeks, so you may decide to create separate tables for these facts. In other cases, multiple fact tables exist because they improve performance. For example, multiple fact tables are often used to hold various levels of aggregated data, particularly when the amount of aggregation is large. An example of multiple fact tables being used for aggregation would be different tables for daily sales, monthly sales, and yearly sales. Creating different tables for different levels of aggregation is a common design technique for a data warehouse database so that any single request is against a table of reasonable size.

Figure 7–3 illustrates the Sales database with an additional fact table for the previous year's sales.

Another use of a fact table is to define a many-to-many relationship between certain dimensions of the business; this type of table is typically known as an associative table. For example, in the Sales database, each product belongs to one or more groups, and each group contains multiple products. A many-to-many relationship is modeled by establishing a fact table that defines the possible combinations of products and groups. To say it another way, a new fact table is being created

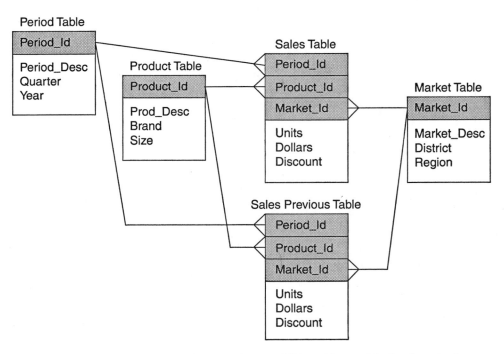

FIGURE 7–3. A sales database with an additional fact table for the previous year's sales.

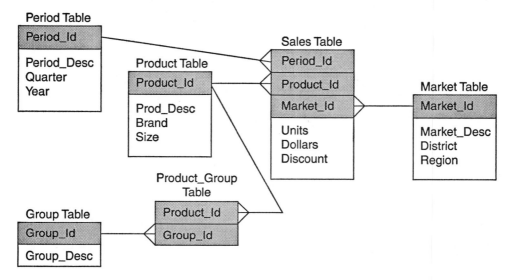

FIGURE 7–4. Another use of a fact table is as an associative table to resolve a many-to-many relationship between groups and products.

to reconcile a many-to-many relationship between different dimensions as shown in Figure 7–4.

Outboard Tables

Dimension tables can also contain a foreign key that references the primary key in another dimension table. The referenced dimension tables are sometimes referred to as outboard, outrigger, or secondary dimension tables. Figure 7–5 includes two outboard tables, District and Region, which define the ID codes used in the Market table.

Variations of a Star Schema

As data access tools mature, the distance between the end user and the physical database structures increases. (Data access

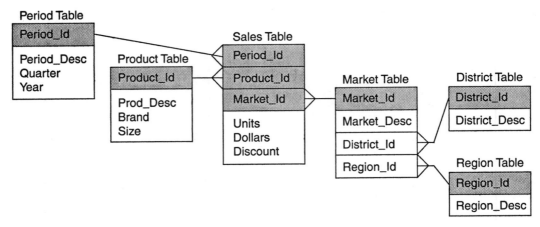

FIGURE 7–5.   An example of secondary dimension (or outboard) tables.

tools are discussed in depth in Chapter 8.) This provides for more flexibility in your physical design. One variation of a star structure is to store all of your dimensional information in third normal form, while keeping your fact table structures the same. This type of star schema is sometimes referred to as a "snowflake" schema. While this sounds like a new concept, it is really a simple variation on the basic star schema that we have been talking about. The two common reasons for the interest in this variation are (1) the emergence of advanced decision support tools that can fully exploit this type of structure, and (2) that many IS organizations feel more comfortable with a design in third normal form. Keep in mind that if your users will be working directly with the physical table structures, you should limit the total number of tables to minimize confusion.

Figure 7–6 shows the database structure from Figure 7–5 with completely denormalized dimension tables. In this example, you end up with a total of nine separate dimensional tables.

This is not an unreasonable structure. However, consider the ramifications of using a customer table with 200 different characteristics. It is unreasonable to create 200 separate tables

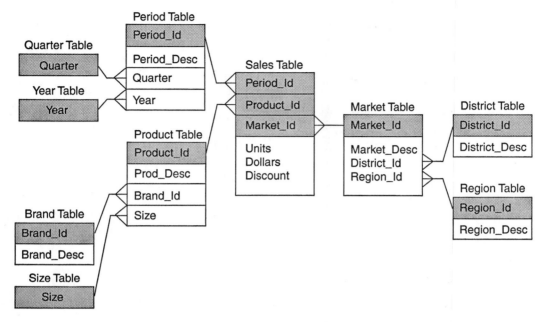

FIGURE 7–6.   A snowflake schema.

for the dimension to be in third normal form. While there are some proponents who advocate a pure approach from one end of the spectrum or the other, a more realistic situation is somewhere in between. A realistic example including denormalized dimensional tables is in Figure 7–15, Putting It All Together, which is at the end of this chapter.

Multi-Star Schemas

In a simple star schema, the primary key in the fact table is formed by concatenating the foreign key columns. In some applications, however, the concatenated foreign keys might not provide a unique identifier for each row in the fact table. These applications require a multi-star schema.

In a multi-star schema, the fact table has both a set of foreign keys, which reference dimension tables, and a primary key, which is composed of one or more columns that provide a unique identifier for each row. The primary key and the foreign keys are not identical in a multi-star schema. This is what distinguishes a multi-star schema from a single-star schema.

Figure 7–7 illustrates the relationship of the fact and dimension tables within a multi-star schema. In the fact table, the foreign keys are Fkey1, Fkey2, and Fkey3, each of which is the primary key in a dimension table. Unlike the simple star schema, these columns do not form the primary key in the fact table. Instead, the two columns Key1 and Key2, which do not reference any dimension tables, and Fkey1 are concatenated to form the primary key. Note that the primary key can be composed of any combination of foreign key and other key columns in a multi-star schema.

Figure 7–8 illustrates a retail sales database designed as a multi-star schema with two outboard tables. This multi-star schema was used because the foreign keys, Store_Id and SKU_Id are not enough to unequally identify a row within the transaction table. The fact table records daily sales in a rolling seven-day database. The primary key for the fact table consists of the four columns Store_Id, Date, Receipt, and Line_item.

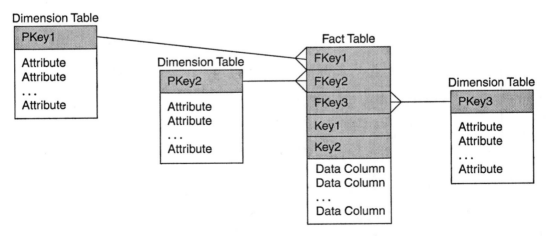

FIGURE 7–7.   A multi-star schema design.

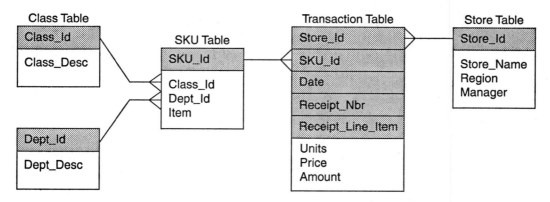

FIGURE 7–8.   Retail sales database designed as a multi-star schema with two secondary dimension tables.

These keys provide the unique identifier for each row. The foreign keys are the columns for Store_Id and SKU_Id, which reference the SKU (Stock Keeping Unit) and Store dimension tables. Two outboard tables, Class and Department, are also being referenced by the SKU dimension table.

Notice that in a multi-star schema, unlike a simple star schema, the same value for the concatenated foreign key in the fact table can occur in multiple rows, so that the concatenated foreign key no longer uniquely identifies each row. For example, in this case the same store (Store_Id) might have multiple sales of the same item (SKU_Id) on the same day (Date). Instead, row identification is based on the primary key(s)—each row is uniquely identified by Date, Receipt, and Line_Item.

A SALAD DRESSING EXAMPLE

This example illustrates how the schema design affects both usability and usefulness of the database.

This database tracks the sales of salad dressing products in supermarkets at weekly intervals over a four-year period and is a typical consumer-goods marketing database.

■ The salad dressing product category contains 14,000 items at the universal product code (UPC) level.

■ Data is summarized for each of 120 geographic areas (markets) in the United States.

■ Data is also summarized for each of 208 weekly time periods spanning four years.

The salad dressing database has one fact table, Sales, and three dimension tables: Product, Week, and Market, as illustrated in Figure 7–9.

Each record in the Sales fact table contains a field for each of the three dimensions: product, period, and market. The columns in the Sales table containing these fields are the foreign keys whose concatenated values give each row in the Sales table a unique identifier. This is therefore a simple star schema. The Sales table also contains seven additional fields that contain values for measures of interest to market analysts.

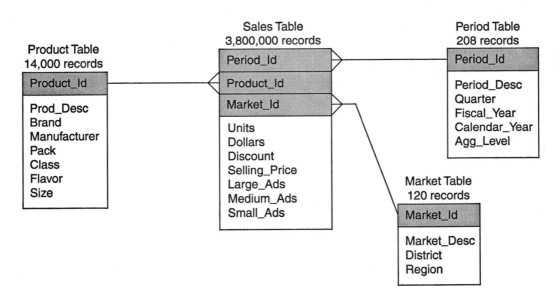

FIGURE 7–9. A salad dressing database with a simple star schema.

Each dimension table describes a business dimension and contains one primary key and some attribute columns for that dimension.

Understanding the Available Data, Browsing the Dimension Tables

To write effective queries, a user needs to be familiar with the contents of the database. A convenient way to find the range of values for a specific dimension is to query the dimension table for that dimension. For example, to see what the markets are for the sales data, a user can enter:

```
SELECT market_desc FROM market
```

to display a list of all the markets, 120 in this case. Similar queries on the product and period tables provide the user with lists of the products and periods covered in the Sales table.

Wildcard expressions can be used to narrow down the browse list to items that approximate those of interest. For example, if the user is interested in ranch-style dressings, a wildcard expression incorporating "ranch" into the SELECT statement limits the browse list from the product table to the appropriate ranch products. This creates a more workable subset of data by limiting the full 14,000 items of the table.

Browsing through the dimension tables is quicker than issuing a SELECT DISTINCT statement on a fact table, especially if the fact table contains millions of rows of data. Having tables of data that define each dimension of the star schema makes this type of browsing activity possible. Users can browse the dimensions of the database using the dimension tables to become familiar with the data contents.

After creating browse lists to understand which dimensions are being addressed in the database design, the user can review these lists to find which markets, products, and time periods they have a particular interest in. The browse lists return the exact descriptions and spellings, making it easier to write the query constraints correctly.

Using Table Attributes

Non-key columns in a dimension table are referred to as attributes. To see how attributes are used, consider the product table for the salad dressing database. It has 14,000 items that are identified by their universal product code (UPC), which provides the primary key (Product_Id). This identifier allows a user to retrieve a unique row. Usually, however, the user does not want data at the UPC level but is interested in higher-level categories such as brand or manufacturer. Additional attributes in the dimension tables permit commonly accessed subsets of an entire group to be differentiated.

For example, the brand attribute allows the 14,000 salad dressing products to be differentiated by brand so that a user can select only products with a specific brand name. Another attribute allows those same 14,000 products to be differentiated by manufacturer. A user analyzing the salad dressing sales could use the attributes Class, Flavor, Size, and Manufacturer from the Product table to select diet ranch salad dressings in 12-ounce bottles from major manufacturers.

Creating Attribute Hierarchies

Viewing data through different, but closely related, perspectives allows the end user to analyze data to the level of detail that is necessary to provide answers. Viewing data from a high level through different dimensions to a more detailed view of data is called drilling down. Viewing data from the detail level up to a summarized, or higher level, is called rolling up. Your database design and the granularity level of the data will determine your ability to drill down or roll up.

End users often wish to see different perspectives on the same data. For instance, you might view sales volume for a particular product across the country, then break up the country by region. Reviewing regional information may show a sales inconsistency that you would like more information on, so you drill down to sales territories that make up the regional data to see where sales may be slipping. Drilling down through the data this way allows you to get closer to a more detailed level of data.

A well-designed star schema will encompass these hierarchies within the dimension tables. Multiple hierarchies can also be represented in a single table. In a table recording information about geographic areas, for example, separate geographic hierarchies–one for physical geography and one for sales organization geography (they are often different) can be represented in the same table. Any of these attributes can then form a basis for constraints. Figure 7–10 shows multiple attribute hierarchies within a dimension that are used for drill-downs and roll-ups of data.

A star schema design that contains complete, consistent, and well-thought-out attribute fields provides users with views of data they can inherently understand and use. A good star schema design helps users write queries that they intuitively

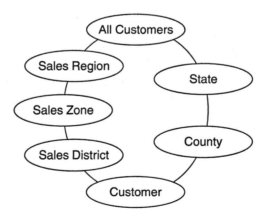

FIGURE 7–10.   Multiple hierarchies within a dimension.

understand and reduces the support burden on the organization responsible for database management.

AGGREGATION

Aggregation is the process of accumulating fact data along predefined attributes. For instance, you can create a summary of dollar sales by region and department by accumulating dollar sales from the store and item level of detail. Within the context of database design, you must make decisions about creating aggregates during the data transformation process and loading the precalculated data into the data warehouse.

The primary driving factors for creating prestored aggregates are to:

■ Improve end user query performance.
■ Reduce the total number of CPU cycles used.

It does not make sense to prestore a specific aggregate that takes two hours to create if it is requested by one user once a year. On the other hand, if that same aggregate is requested by 300 users on a daily basis this processing could adversely affect your operational systems. In this case, prestored aggregates would be warranted. You should create the prestored aggregate once during the data transformation process and load it into the database. Figure 7–11 shows prestored aggregate tables across both the geography and product dimensions.

It may not be necessary to prestore every combination of the attributes. To determine what to prestore in your data warehouse, you need to consider not only the frequency of end user access but also the potential reduction in total number of rows. For example, in the tables shown in Figure 7–12, you may have a fact table that has 10,000,000 rows of data at the store and item level of detail. If you aggregate to the item region level of detail, you may end up with 9,000,000 rows of data. However, if you aggregate to the market and item level of detail, you

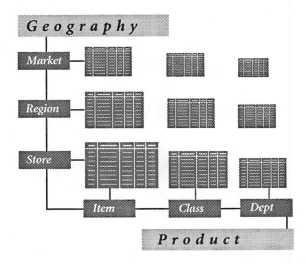

FIGURE 7–11.   Prestored aggregate tables across both the geography and product dimensions.

have only 1,000,000 rows. In this case, do not store item region data, but keep the item market data. Summarizing data only at selected levels is referred to as sparse aggregation. By selecting appropriate aggregation levels, you can optimize both query performance and disk storage within your data warehouse.

One final concept to note is that when loading a data warehouse, you still need to use classic database techniques such as physical table partitioning. This becomes very important with data warehouses having hundreds of gigabytes of data. An example of how partitioning would be included in your aggregation strategy is shown in Figure 7–13, where only the largest aggregate fact tables are partitioned.

DENORMALIZATION

Denormalization is the process of combining tables in a careful and thoughtful manner to improve performance. This is really the process of breaking the rules for third normal form. The primary reasons to do this are:

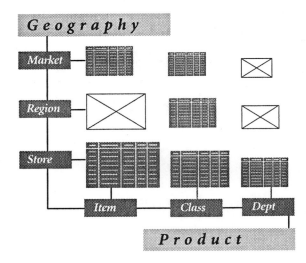

FIGURE 7–12. Sparse aggregation across both the geography and product dimensions.

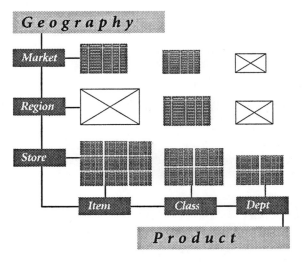

FIGURE 7–13. Sparse aggregation with physical partitioning at the store level of detail.

■ To reduce the number of joins that must be processed in your average queries, thereby improving database performance.

■ To map the physical database structure more closely to the user's Dimensional Business Model. Again, structuring your tables along the lines of how users will ask questions will provide you the opportunity to tune for common access paths which will again improve performance.

Over the last several years, data warehouse developers have fine tuned denormalization techniques, resulting in the entire star schema approach.

DATA WAREHOUSE DATABASE DESIGN EXAMPLES

A series of specific examples will show how the many different concepts discussed in this chapter are applied in the real world.

Reservation Database

Figure 7–14 illustrates a multi-star schema, in which the primary and foreign keys are not composed of the same set of columns. This design also contains a family of fact tables: a Bookings table, an Actuals table, and a Promotion table.

This database tracks reservations (bookings) and actual accommodations rented for a chain of hotels, as well as various promotions. It also maintains information about customers, promotions, and each hotel in the chain.

Investment Database

Figure 7–15 is an example of a database that tracks sales of investment funds on a daily and monthly basis. It also maintains information about the client organizations, the investment funds, and various trading programs.

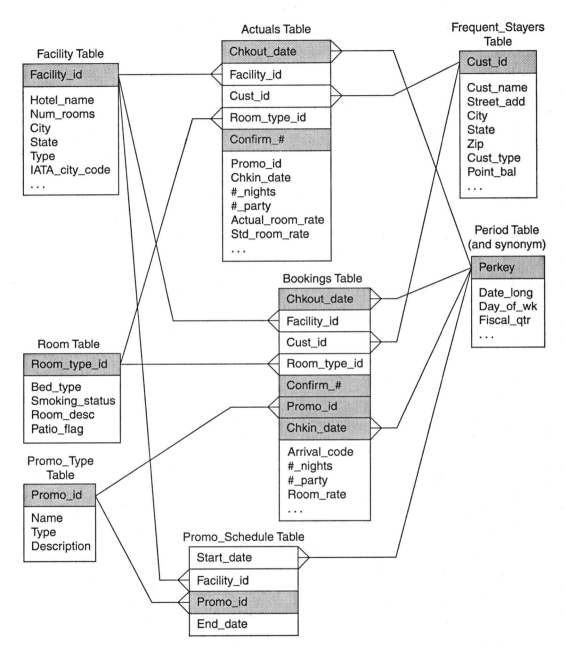

FIGURE 7–14.   A multi-star schema design for a reservation system.

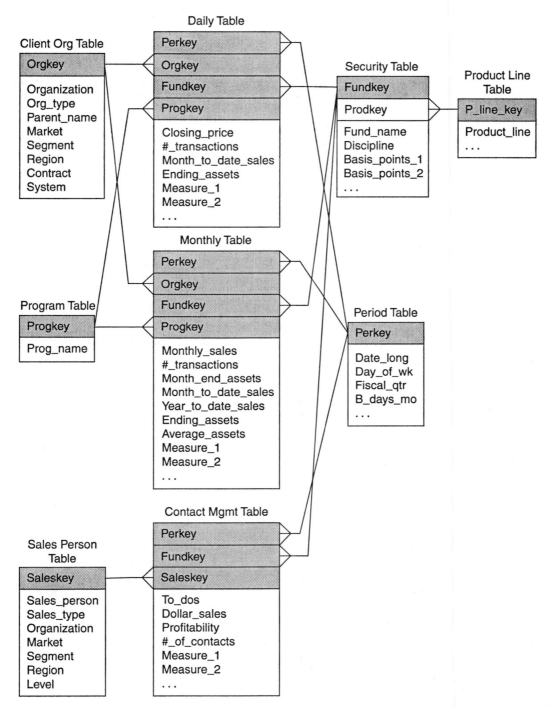

FIGURE 7–15. A simple star schema design for an investment system. Daily data is stored in one table and aggregated data is stored in another table.

This example illustrates a simple schema to handle aggregations. In this case, daily data is stored in one table and aggregated data in another, rather than combining both levels of aggregation in one table. The ratio of aggregated data to nonaggregated data and knowledge of the expected queries can help determine whether to combine various aggregation levels in a single database or use multiple tables. If aggregated and nonaggregated data are stored in the same table, each query must always specify the level of aggregation as a constraint.

Health Insurance Database

A simple star schema for a health care insurer used for claims analysis is illustrated in Figure 7–16. This database records policy sales and claims and maintains records of customers and their policies and claims against those policies.

Putting It All Together

Figure 7–17 displays a more realistic example of the many concepts that have been discussed throughout this chapter.

SUMMARY

In this chapter, you should have learned the following:

■ The goals of a decision support system are often achieved by a database design called a star schema, a simple structure with relatively few tables and well defined join paths.

The benefits of using star schema database design for a data warehouse include:

■ Creating a database design providing fast response times.

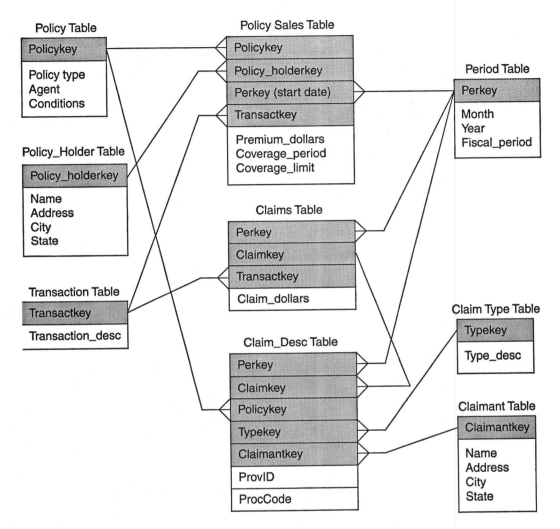

FIGURE 7–16.   A simple star schema for a health care insurer.

- Providing a design which can easily be modified or added to throughout development iterations, and as the data warehouse grows.

- Paralleling, in the database design, how the end users customarily think of and use the data.

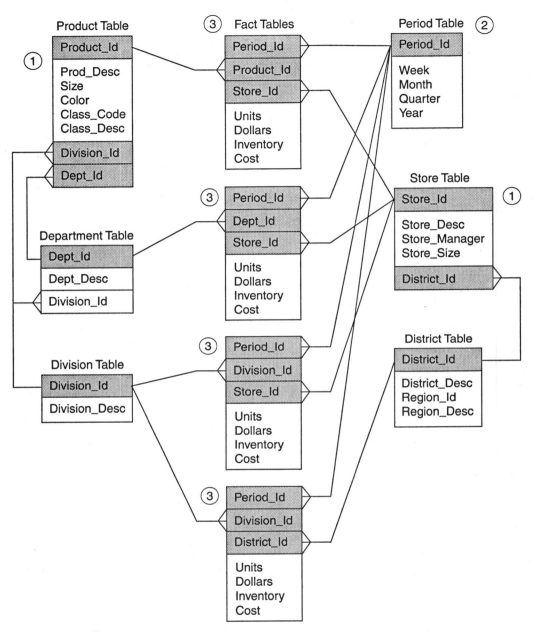

| Product Table | Fact Tables ③ | Period Table ② |

Product Table ①
- Product_Id
- Prod_Desc
- Size
- Color
- Class_Code
- Class_Desc
- Division_Id
- Dept_Id

Fact Tables ③
- Period_Id
- Product_Id
- Store_Id
- Units
- Dollars
- Inventory
- Cost

Period Table ②
- Period_Id
- Week
- Month
- Quarter
- Year

Department Table
- Dept_Id
- Dept_Desc
- Division_Id

③
- Period_Id
- Dept_Id
- Store_Id
- Units
- Dollars
- Inventory
- Cost

Store Table ①
- Store_Id
- Store_Desc
- Store_Manager
- Store_Size
- District_Id

Division Table
- Division_Id
- Division_Desc

③
- Period_Id
- Division_Id
- Store_Id
- Units
- Dollars
- Inventory
- Cost

District Table
- District_Id
- District_Desc
- Region_Id
- Region_Desc

③
- Period_Id
- Division_Id
- District_Id
- Units
- Dollars
- Inventory
- Cost

① The Store and the Product Dimensions have been partially denormalized.

② The Period Dimension is fully denormalized.

③ The fact tables are split out by aggregation level.

FIGURE 7–17. Putting it all together—a more realistic retail star schema.

■ Simplifying the understanding and navigation of metadata for both developers and end users.

■ Broadening the choices of front end data access tools, as some products require a star schema design.

■ A star schema contains two types of tables, fact tables and dimension tables.

■ Fact tables contain quantitative or factual data about a business—the information being queried. Dimension tables hold descriptive data that reflects the dimensions of the business.

■ In a simple star schema, the primary key for the fact table is composed of the foreign keys from the dimension tables.

■ A star schema can, and often does, contain multiple fact tables.

■ In schemas where the concatenated foreign keys from the dimension tables do not provide a unique identifier, a multi-star schema will be used. In a multi-star schema, the fact table has both a set of foreign keys referencing the dimensions, and a primary key to provide a unique identifier for each row.

■ Dimensions often contain business hierarchies, view data through different, but closely related perspectives and to allow users to drill up and down to the level of detail necessary to provide answers.

■ Aggregation is accumulating fact data along predefined attributes. Aggregated data that is requested by users on a daily basis will often be precalculated and loaded into the data warehouse to improve end user query performance and reduce the number of CPU cycles used.

■ The determination of which aggregates should be prestored will be based on the frequency of end user access, as well as the potential reduction in the total number of rows returned from a query.

Chapter 8

Successful Data Access

GENERAL UNDERSTANDING OF DATA ACCESS

With a goal of providing information to users, front end data access to your data warehouse becomes one of the most important aspects of building a data warehouse. Experience shows that the tool or tools selected can make or break your data warehouse. Unfortunately, the selection of the front end tool is often left until the warehouse is nearly complete. Information on what tools are available and what type of data warehouses they support is important to understand before you design your warehouse.

You need to think about setting up an environment to support data access and analysis rather than just selecting a front end software package. This environment includes not only the software itself, but the training, end user support, and development of *predefined DSS applications*. It is important to realize that a DSS application is not the same thing as a COBOL program. A DSS application can, in general, be considered one or more predefined reports where users may or may not have the ability to provide input parameters.

As you begin to look at data access software that is on the market, do not underestimate the sophistication and complexity of this type of software. You need to make sure that you allow enough time and apply enough resources to really understand what you need and which tools can meet your requirements. In general, the selection of a tool can take several weeks, but keep in mind that the development of DSS applications will be much shorter than traditional application development.

WHAT ARE YOU REALLY TRYING TO DO?

You must review the overall goals for your data warehouse again when you begin your search for tools. You should step back and ask:

- What are you trying to do?
- Do you plan to be in the business of software development or are you trying to support the business?

- Are you planning to deliver reports electronically or are you planning to deliver analytical capabilities?
- Are you looking to replace the creation and delivery of all existing hard copy reports or are your users clamoring to have data they need at their fingertips to make better business decisions?

The in-house development of full data software is not recommended. Even if you are able to develop an initial application quickly, the maintenance and enhancements to this application are usually extremely costly over time. Many software companies are dedicated to delivering this capability to the marketplace. These organizations are investing hundreds of person years into the development and maintenance of these tools, which have sophisticated analytical capabilities. Realistically, the effort to develop this type of tool will most likely exceed your schedule as well as your budget.

TYPES OF ACCESS

How do people receive information from the data warehouse? The most common ways are:

- *Parameter-based ad hoc report:* Fixed report formats where the user can change the parameters. For example, the end user may be able to specify the time period or the products to be included in the report. The end user may also have the ability to further manipulate the results. Often, end users have the ability to copy an existing report to modify it for a specific purpose. While the user is really creating a new report, it is not from scratch, but rather from tweaking existing reports.
- *Electronic access to predefined reports:* Predefined fixed format reports are generated and placed in a commonly accessible location for users to pull up for viewing as needed.

■ *Full ad hoc analysis:* The user interacts directly with the tool to create a brand new analysis from scratch. This is also sometimes referred to as ad hoc reporting. It is important to make sure that everyone on your project team and within your targeted user base has a common definition of ad hoc. Since ad hoc has rather customized definitions, you should also clarify with external vendors or groups what their definition of ad hoc is.

■ *Hard copy reports:* Predefined fixed format reports are generated, printed, and then delivered to the user.

There are a variety of ways that end users can navigate through the system to use it. The primary interface methods are:

■ *Executive information system:* Provides big button navigation along predefined paths to access predefined analysis.

■ *Structured decision support:* Provides big button navigation along predefined paths to access predefined and ad hoc reports. The users have further analytical capabilities available once a report was retrieved.

■ *Unstructured decision support:* Provides access to all predefined and ad hoc reports. The navigation to get to the specific reports is unstructured. The full range of tool capabilities is available to the user, including building new analyses from scratch.

LEVELS OF USERS

Not all business professionals have the same data and analytical requirements. Contrary to popular opinion, most business professionals will not develop their own reports. This is due to a combination of technical skill level and pure analytical requirements. Let's review the broad spectrum of users.

■ *Executive User:*   Wants easy-to-access status of the corporation. Needs predefined sets of reports that can be easily located through navigation of menus. Tends to prefer big buttons that refer to business functions. Wants results displayed graphically, with support details as needed. Basic additional analysis may be desired, but often the next step would be to make a phone call or send an e-mail to the appropriate person or department.

■ *Novice / Casual User:*   Someone who needs access to information on an occasional basis. Will not be logged on daily, or in some cases even weekly. Due to the length of time between sessions, big button navigation is also required here. Wants to step through predefined analysis. This type of user may also be interested in setting parameters to run any report at that moment. Prompting of choices will be critical for this user.

■ *Business Analyst:*   One of a large number of end users who use information daily, but do not have (and don't necessarily want to have) the technical knowledge to build reports completely from scratch. This user may find predefined navigation paths helpful initially, and may progress to wanting to go directly to the report of choice. This user will regularly change parameters and look at the results many different ways. He or she will want to modify existing reports to customize them to meet a specific need, but will generally not want to start from scratch.

■ *Power User:*   The business professional who loves technology. This type of user tends to be the type who currently writes his or her own macros and may work with PCs at home. This type of user will want to change parameters and manipulate result sets, and is comfortable starting with a clean slate and creating his or her own reports/analyses. Power users want to be able to write their own macros and often place result sets into end user tools such as Lotus 1-2-3 (although this may no longer be necessary after you finish building your data warehouse). The power user often develops reports that can then be shared with others in the organization.

■ *Application Developer:*   Differences between a power user and application developer are often minor. Usually, the application developer's primary responsibilities are to support the business, rather than having actual business responsibilities also. The application developer will be trained to not only create reports/analyses for use by others but will be a driving force in setting standards, such as where and how reports will be named and located. The application developer will often also be highly focused on performance optimization of the reports.

Every organization has one of the above types of users. You will find them across a continuum of experience and business units. The key here is to understand the characteristics of your target audience and relate these back to your choices in data access tool. Figure 8–1 summarizes the types of users and their warehouse usage.

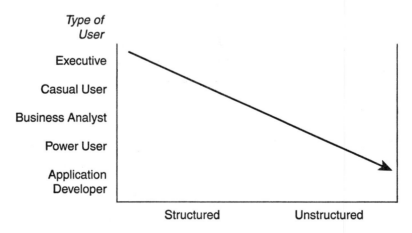

FIGURE 8–1.   Users and types of access.

WHAT IS A DSS APPLICATION?

If you build one, they will come.

This is one of the most common myths surrounding data warehouses, and it is NOT true. The idea that simply loading the data will allow your users to gain business knowledge is an unrealistic view of a data warehouse. Likewise, simply making a front end access tool available will not ensure success.

Data access tools are much too sophisticated for many business professionals to use right out of the box. Due to the complexity and breadth of the capabilities, even power users will have to progress along a rather steep learning curve. *Keep in mind that many of these tools are not designed to make easy tasks easier, but rather to make complex tasks doable.* The key to helping users along the learning curve is to provide structured or free form navigation paths to a set of predefined reports and analyses. These predefined reports are considered the beginning of a DSS application.

We have established the need for many users in an organization to use prebuilt reports and analyses. Who develops these? How are they developed? The data warehouse project needs to accommodate both the time required and funding to support the development of these predefined reports. You must remember that this is a starter set. Do not spec out 100 reports. Define the top ten to twelve analyses that will be required. Keep in mind that a single DSS "report" can yield hundreds of final reports by changing the constraints and/or level of aggregation or detail displayed.

Also, be aware that you will not necessarily be able to predetermine which reports will be the most valuable to your users. Take a first cut at it, and then work closely with the users. Looking at the core reports six months after initial development, you may not see any of the the original reports. This is evidence of a successful system at work.

DATA ACCESS CHARACTERISTICS

Before jumping right into a description of what you can buy today, we must provide a background explaining what capabilities are possible across a spectrum of software products. After you know what can be done, then we will review how different classes of software products address these capabilities.

How you access data follows several general steps. These fundamental functions will exist for ALL data access tools to some degree. In addition to data access, more advanced analytical capabilities also fall into several general categories. A description of each will be provided.

Summary of Data Access and Analysis
Visualization of the data warehouse
User formulates request
The request is processed
Presentation of results
Advanced analytics
Communicate findings

Visualization of the Data Warehouse

Users must be presented with the contents of the data warehouse. On the simple end, a list of tables and columns is all that is displayed. Advancing along the sophistication spectrum, presenting the tables and columns using business terms, provide full dimensional viewpoint of the database—where user never interacts directly with tables structures.

User Formulates Request

The full spectrum of capabilities ranges from manually writing SQL statements to drag and drop from a list of available tables and columns to complete multidimensional analysis where the user works completely with business terms, information is organized along business hierarchies, and drag and drop capabilities are used to create a request. A request really is comprised of two basics: what data you want (the constraints) and how you want to see it, including level of detail.

Viewing the Results.   You need to be able to specify the general format of the returned data. Tabular or cross-tabular formats are most common. Business professionals think in terms of cross-tabular formats—rows and columns.

- The general row and column information needs to be specified. I want product information down the side and weeks across the top.
- The level of detail to look at is also important to specify. I want to see item detail by week.
- The specific facts or metrics also need to be selected.

There are several different types of metrics that may be supported by a data access tools. Each type is discussed here.

Metrics and Calculated Metrics

Simple metrics: The retrieval of columns of data that are physically stored in the data warehouse is the simplest type of metric. Common simple metrics are Sales Dollars and Units Sold.

Calculated metrics: Metrics that are the result of performing standard mathematical calculations upon simple metrics are considered calculated or derived metrics. Examples include average retail price, which is Dollars Sales divided by Units Sold. Also a simple projection of a 15 percent increase in sales can be calculated as Dollar Sales multiplied by 1.15.

Advanced dimensional metrics: This type of calculation requires data from multiple levels within the data hierarchies. For example, Brand Share of Category requires applying two sets of selection criteria—what brands and what is the associated category. The calculation is Brand Sales divided by Category Sales. Other common examples include penetration and contribution. *These calculations cannot be performed with a single SQL statement.*

Transformation metrics: This type of metric requires that you pull information for one specified set of criteria and for a related criteria set to compare them. The most common example of a transformation metric is *time comparison analysis* such as comparing this year versus last year sales performance. The current period of sales is selected, then the related prior year is determined (the original date is transformed to the prior year). The prior year sales can then be retrieved. Finally, the variance between the two can be calculated. Another example is to compare store sales with other stores of a comparable background. This calculation also requires the transformation of a specific store into the related stores, so that the appropriate sales data can be retrieved. *These calculations cannot be performed with one SQL statement.*

Aggregation: How will the tool determine access to prestored aggregation and/or when to create the aggregate on the fly? It is also important to understand where the aggregation will occur—at the client workstation, the RDBMS, or somewhere else? There are two types of aggregation that can occur:

- *Straight aggregation:* Accumulate information along the hierarchies and attributes within the data model. For example, items roll up to sizes, classes, and departments. This is usually the type of aggregate that is prestored in the database.

- *Custom aggregation:* Accumulate information along nonstandard paths. For example, aggregate all of the items in a brand except for sample sizes, or aggregate to a specific list of markets that you have determined to use as test markets.

Row math: Provide the same mathematical capabilities to perform calculations between rows in the database as is often seen with financial data. SQL does not support this type of calculation today. A common example of this requirement is when actual and budget information are stored in the same table as separate rows, distinguished by a Type Key. Most users want to see actual, budget, and variance information on the same report. Some tools support this type of analysis, others don't.

Nonaggregatable data: How do you handle nonsummable measures? Or enable the analysis of stock metrics such as inventory levels, turnover, sell through, and reorder quantities? You must set up rules to handle this type of data; for instance, it does not make sense to aggregate the current inventory level over time periods.

Constraining a Request. Constraining a request specifies what slice of the data warehouse is to be selected. The ability to constrain should include:

- Constraining a specific column to a value using basic operators (<, >, =, <>...).

■ Specification of the time dimension. You can constrain upon specific dates that are stored in a lookup table, or you may need to use dynamic data definitions which are defined relative to a changing date. For example, return to me all of the data from for the last two weeks. This date calculation is between (today—2 weeks) and today. This type of constraint changes over time rather than being a hard coded value.

■ Constraints that may also be required against metrics. For example, return for me all of the products where the difference between actual and planned sales is less than 0.

■ Constraints for future use saved. Advanced tools allow you to combine collections of constraints using full set mathematics (intersection, union, not).

■ The ability to automatically prompt a user for constraint values. You may want to prompt for only one or two variables (which region and which month) or you may want to prompt for all variables (which geography, customer, time period, and product).

How the Request Is Processed

Once a user has formulated a request, the tool must fulfill the request and return the appropriate answer set.

All tools that use precoded SQL pass the statement directly to the RDBMS (most tools use ODBC as a vehicle for communication, others may use different paths).

More sophisticated tools translate the end user's request to generate the appropriate SQL statement(s), and then pass the request along. You should understand how advanced metrics are being calculated. Are they created with multiple SQL statements or is there a programmatic process that operates on the base data itself?

The multidimensional tools will translate the end user request into the required language to retrieve the result set from the MDBMS.

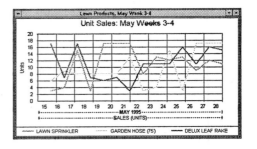

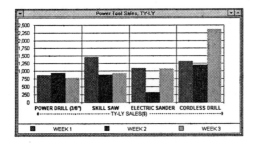

FIGURE 8–2. Various presentations of results. *(Courtesy of MicroStrategy, Inc.)*

Promotional Items Inventory Analysis		Boston			
		Sales (Units)	Avg Inventory	Turnover (Days)	Sell Through
Power Tools	Skill Saw	181	62	19	80%
	Electric Sander	312	71	11	70%
	Cordless Drill	295	60	12	73%
Hand Tools	Handi Screwdriver Set	365	67	9	81%
	Rachet Kit (74 Piece)	264	65	13	40%
	Adjustable Wrench Set	365	66	10	65%
	Hammer (24oz.)	273	75	13	92%
Electrical	Romex Wire (3 Strand)	341	71	10	67%
	Wall Switches (White)	316	67	11	84%
	Outlets (White)	293	63	12	43%

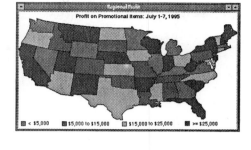

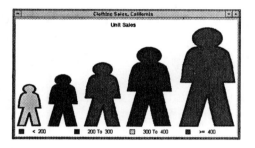

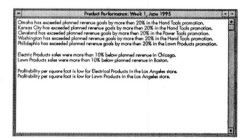

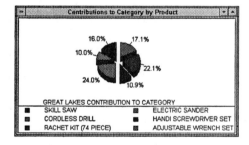

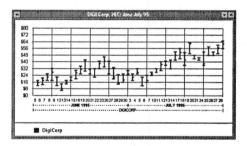

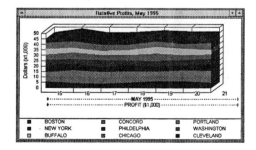

FIGURE 8–2. *Continued*

Presentation of Results

Data returned from a request can be displayed in a wide variety of ways. All are designed to assist a user in gathering insights from the data. Samples of how information can be presented are illustrated in Figure 8–2.

Reports.   Reports can take two major forms:

- Columnar format (basic format returned directly from an SQL statement).
- Crosstab format supporting multidimensional views of the data.

Once a report is presented, a wide range of capabilities may allow modification of the display, including:

- Changing the axis of the report (swap rows and columns).
- Changing the sort order of the results.
- Adding subtotals and grand totals at appropriate breaks in the reports.
- Creating stoplight-style thresholds (basic red, green, and yellow colors on the report to indicate ranges of values).
- Formatting of fonts, styles, sizes, and colors.

Graphs.   Graphical display of information allows easy detection of trends and anomalies. A wide variety of graph types is often available, including:

- Line
- Two- or three-dimensional bar
- Stacked bar
- Pie
- Scatter
- Bubble

- Tape
- Area
- Hi/lo/close
- Log

Within a graphical display, users may be able to change:

- Graph type
- Axis labels
- Colors
- Titles

Maps. Mapping capabilities allow the presentation of information to expand beyond grids and graphs into the world of user-defined objects. Mapping provides a powerful method for displaying analyses that contain a geographic dimension. Both a high-level summary of the result set and the low-level details can be readily communicated through this pictorial format.

Communicate Findings

A DSS is not a standalone system. The results of any given analysis may be included in a formal presentation (slide show), e-mailed to management or appropriate team members, and otherwise shared throughout the company. No software tool lives on its own. The tool needs to interact with other personal productivity tools such as spread sheet, word processing, and workgroup software.

Advanced Features

Advanced Analytics. Beyond these fundamental steps, there are some more advanced capabilities that many organizations require to support the full decision making process. These may include:

■ Exception reporting: Alerts are headline messages that appear when user-defined conditions are met or when there is a problem.

■ Drill down: Users have the freedom to "drive off" the existing report and retrieve information that may lie along, above, or below the current level of detail. Drill down can be done from a report or a graph.

■ Data surfing: You can keep the report layout constant but change the constraints. For example, a sales trend report for basketballs in the northeast, changing to a sales trend report for shoes in the far west. Data surfing also allows you to keep the constraints constant but vary the report. For example, continue to look at shoes in the far west, but for an inventory status report instead of the sales trend.

■ Ranking: Review information that is ranked on one or more columns.

■ Automation: Mechanisms are in place to schedule recurring analysis at specified time.

Batch Query Processing.   Batch query processing is the offloading of query processing to free up the end user's workstation for other work. It also is beneficial to support recurring analysis. Users often run analyses on a weekly basis. For example, users may wish to create a group of Monday morning reports that have already run and are waiting for them when they arrive at work. This functionality is really providing the ability to offload and run now, or schedule a specific analysis to run at a specified date and time.

Other benefits that are gained by offloading queries to another server include:

DSS Application Development

The development of a DSS application varies from actual programming to drag-and-drop construction. The fundamental questions to understand are:

- How are reports or analyses shared between users?
- Is programming required or can you create reports and analyses without programming?
- Can you set up libraries of reports?
- How are reports upgraded when new versions are released?
- Do IS application developers use the same development tool as power users?
- How are structured navigation paths or big buttons created?
- A query governor to limit the allowable elapsed time for a query to run or to limit the total number of rows that can be returned.
- Workflow management, to manage the query load against the database.
- The ability to run a query during off-peak hours, and for less cost.

CLASSES OF TOOLS

Now that you have an understanding of the types of things that you may be able to accomplish with a DSS tool, it is important to understand the classes of tools that are actively being marketed today. There are five major classifications of tools. An overview of each will be provided.

Data Access/Query Tools

This class of tool provides a graphical user interface to the data warehouse. The user will interact directly with the table structures. Some of these tools may provide a layer of abstraction that allows you to assign business names to the different columns and tables. These tools primarily return data in tabular format and may provide manipulation of the result set. A high level view of query tool architecture is illustrated in Figure 8–3.

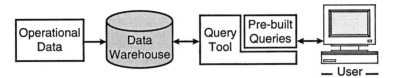

FIGURE 8–3.   Query Tool Architecture.

Report Writers

This class of tool may also provide a layer of abstraction that allows you to assign business names to the different columns and tables. These tools primarily return data in tabular or cross tabular format. These tools provide extensive formatting capabilities to allow you to re-create a report to look a specific way. Again, users tend to have to work closely with the physical table structures. Figure 8–4 shows the architecture of report writers.

Multidimensional Database Management Systems (MDBMS)

This class of tool provides advanced metric support with extensive slice-and-dice capabilities. Multidimensional Database Management Systems (MDBMS) require that data be loaded into the multidimensional databases, as diagrammed in Figure 8–5. The data does not need to be resident in a data warehouse in order to be loaded into a MDBMS, but can come directly from the operational systems. Access to data in a multidimensional database is accomplished via two primary paths. Many

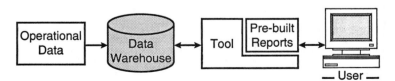

FIGURE 8–4.   Report Writer Architecture.

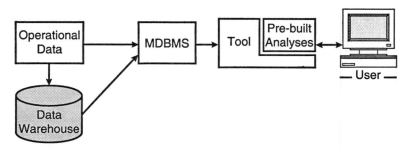

FIGURE 8–5.   Multidimensional Database Management System
Architecture.

of the software packages provide Application Programming Interfaces (APIs) so that you can develop your own front end to tap into the MDBMS. Many MDBMS vendors also provide a suite of graphical data access software or a graphical user interface that can be used to develop end user applications. Some of these tools can technically reach through the MDBMS into a data warehouse to provide further drill down capabilities.

Advanced DSS Tools

A key differentiating characteristic of advanced decision support tools is the ability to provide multidimensional analysis directly against the data warehouse database. These tools are often driven off of shared metadata (see the section on metadata later in this chapter). They support advanced metrics, extensive slice and dice of the data and drilling capabilities. Many also offer batch query support. The architecture of many advanced DSS tools, as shown in Figure 8–6, can be applied to large data warehouses.

Executive Information Systems (EIS)

Historically, Executive Information Systems were created by constructing predefined reports with a structured GUI for navi-

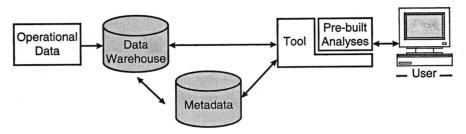

FIGURE 8–6.   Advanced DSS Tool Architecture.

gation. Often, the EIS was completely separate from any decision support system, often with its own database. Today, EIS is viewed more as an extension of a DSS, providing a higher level view of the same information. The EIS of today is often created with the same tool as the DSS.

Tiered Architectures

When researching the more advanced tools, you may hear about multitiered architectures. Tools with multitiered architectures generally work as follows:

- One-tier: The client software and the database reside on the same physical machine.
- Two-tier: The client software and the database reside on two different machines.
- Three-tier: The client software and the database reside on two different machines. The third tier varies dramatically between vendors. The third tiers will be generally be used for one or more of the following:
  - *Computational engine:* The raw data is returned to the middle tier, advanced multidimensional calculations are performed, and the answer is sent back to the users.
  - *Resource manager:* Performs no additional analytical functions from the basic two-tier implementation, but provides the ability to offload work from the client workstation to run in the background, at off hours and

at regularly scheduled times (for example, after new data has been loaded).

- *Multidimensional database:* The multidimensional database itself can be considered a third tier. Data is loaded into the MDBMS from operational systems or the data warehouse and is made available to the end users.

DATA DESIGN REQUIREMENTS

Keep in mind that most of the work you will be doing for the design and population of the data warehouse must be done for any of the classes of tools.

Designing your data warehouse using a star schema will support the broadest possible number of front end tools. If you have already completed development for your data warehouse and you are now looking at tools, do not rule out a tool because you need to make minor modifications to your warehouse. Given the size of the investment in your data warehouse, you want a tool that will perform well. This may require modifications to your data structures. In most cases, if a tool requires a star schema, the only modifications required will be to your dimensional or lookup tables. These tables are usually less than 5 percent of the total size of the database.

METADATA

Operational Metadata versus DSS Metadata

Metadata is data about data. In the world of decision support, there are two primary types of metadata. The first type of metadata contains information about how your operational systems map into your data warehouse. This may include original source system information, field names, and data transformation information. The second type, which we will be focusing on here, is information about how your data warehouse maps to the end user's Dimensional Business Model. This second type of metadata, DSS metadata, provides analysts with a catalog of data in

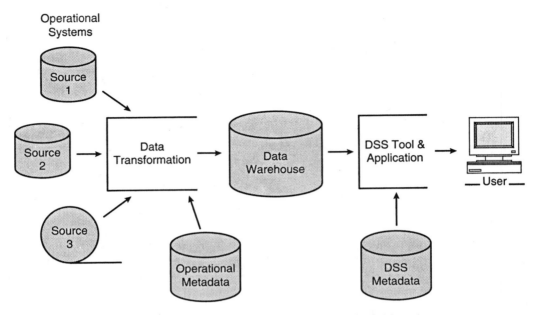

FIGURE 8–7. Operational Metadata and DSS Metadata.

the data warehouse and maps the physical data warehouse to user-friendly Dimensional Business Model as discussed in Chapter 6. Figure 8–7 illustrates both types of metadata.

A well-designed DSS application retrieves hard data from a database and translates it into information meaningful to your business. To do this, the application must understand both the Dimensional Business Model and the location and structure of the data warehouse. Metadata, this data about data, acts as the link from the warehouse and the conceptual business framework to the DSS application.

Warehouse Changes

DSS metadata provides a layer of abstraction between the data warehouse and the reports and analyses. As you change your physical database structure, you only have to update your metadata once and all of the applications will use the new structures. The metadata layer prevents changes to the underlying warehouse from causing the reports and analyses to break down. As a result, evolutionary or architectural changes in the data warehouse can be immediately reflected in your decision support application. For example, if a corporation restructures to eliminate a layer of management, the DSS application should "reconfigure" itself using metadata to reflect the new organizational hierarchy as soon as the data corresponding to the new hierarchy is added to the warehouse.

How Is DSS Metadata Used?

The decision support tool provides the front end user interface to manipulate the metadata and use it to build reports and analyses. The metadata may also contain the information about all of the reports or the DSS application specifics. This allows the graphical user interface (GUI) to drive off the metadata for both ad hoc analysis and prebuilt reports. This technique allows applications to be configured, not custom coded.

Application Deployment

Metadata serves another purpose as well: In large-scale deployments, shared metadata can significantly reduce maintenance costs and update cycles. Applications can be rolled out onto thousands of desktops, with a layer of metadata serving as the link between the client application and the data warehouse. Therefore, when the structure of the warehouse is altered to reflect current business conditions, the shared metadata can be changed centrally by the warehouse administrators, and all the client applications will be updated automatically and transparently. If the warehouse is moved to another location, the data is distributed over multiple warehouses, or if the database software is replaced, the shared metadata allows the end-users to carry on with business as usual with no maintenance and update interruptions.

SELECTING TOOLS FOR YOUR ORGANIZATION

One Tool Fits All?

Historically, no single tool had all of the capabilities to span executive information systems through decision support systems through report writing. As each class of tools matures, the strict lines of delineation are beginning to blur. As you review the tools environment, you must determine what specific class of tool you require.

You will need to set up procedures/infrastructure to evaluate the different tools. In the optimal world, one tool would provide everything and all users would use it. Reality says that many organizations have different target audiences and may indeed consider acquiring multiple tools to meet a spectrum of data access requirements (see the previous section on levels of users).

The Request for Proposal (RFP)

It is common practice to use a request for proposal (RFP) as a vehicle to learn about different products and to reduce the number of products to review in detail. There are some cases where the time and effort to develop and evaluate the results from an RFP can take longer than implementing the tool itself. If your corporate culture requires you to include the RFP as part of the selection process, make sure that you do the following:

- Educate yourself and your team prior to developing the RFP.
- Understand and target a specific class of tool.
- Predetermine the weighting factors for the characteristics.
- Predetermine how you will tabulate responses.
- Use relevant questions.

■ Make your questions specific enough to determine tool differences.

■ Give vendors enough time to do you justice (Giving only a week to respond may not yield the best answers).

■ Be prepared for the responses—Don't be overwhelmed—if you send out a twenty-five page RFP to 15 vendors, you may see 100+ page responses—a total of 1500 pages! Do you have procedures and the time to analyze 1500 pages?

Key Considerations

You need to understand your corporate requirements and how potential tools address those requirements. The primary areas to make sure you understand include:

■ *General architecture requirements:* What infrastructures are currently in place? What are your corporation's future architecture plans?

■ *Scalability requirements:* How big will your data be? How many users will you support? How soon will your warehouse reach those volumes?

■ *Tool requirements:* Is a particular database schema required? Does the tool support prestored and/or on-the-fly aggregation? If so, how?

■ *Implementation:* How do the internals of the tool work? What is set up for you? What do you need to set up? How difficult is it to perform the initial setup? What is required for initial installation?

■ *Support:* How are DSS applications constructed? What will be required to support those applications over time?

■ *Price:* Compare apples to apples and include all the component parts ("per client workstation" prices do not necessarily tell the whole story). Also consider potential volume discounts. What costs are constant regardless of tool (i.e., data preparation)? What do the development and support costs look like over time?

Overall, be sure to gain a realistic understanding of how the "magic"' occurs on the screen.

What Matters to You?

Make sure that you keep the big picture in mind when doing tool selection. If you are in a point-by-point, feature-by-feature battle between multiple tools, you must step back. Does is really matter if you have ten versus twelve color graphs available to you? Keep a broad corporatewide perspective.

Many of the most visible components of a tool are the easiest to change. With today's advancements in GUI, you may find that the differences may only be who compiled using the latest VBX. So, while the interface is important, it is by no means the most important feature in selecting a tool.

A much more important consideration is the fundamental architecture issues. These are what differentiate the various products and will also be the hardest to change over time.

Selecting a Vendor Not Just a Tool

As you begin to narrow down your list of possible tools, make sure that you take the time to understand the vendor's corporate vision and the future direction of that company. What are the product plans for the immediate, mid- and long-term? What is the vendor's track record for delivering high-quality releases on schedule? How much do you want to be able to influence the next releases? How willing is the vendor to partner with you for development and/or enhancement/design input?

If you have external consultants involved in your data warehouse development and tools selection, make sure you know their knowledge levels of the tools. You should also be aware of their vendor relationships, business alliances, and biases because these may substantially affect your options. You need to stay involved in the process too—someone from your organization should be speaking directly with the vendors. (Remember the game telephone as a child?) Additionally, be sure to ask for and call references from other companies that are actively using the product.

SUMMARY

In this chapter, you should have learned the following:

- An understanding of what tools are available and what types of data warehouses they support is important to understand before you design your warehouse.
- An environment for data access includes the data access software, training, support, and a starter set of applications to enable users to access information from your data warehouse.
- Do not underestimate the sophistication of tools currently on the market; these tools may have a long learning curve, so be prepared to support this.
- The in-house development of a front end data access tool is not highly recommended; maintenance and enhancement costs could far exceed your schedule and budget.
- The levels of users should always be a major consideration in choosing a data acccess tool.
- The idea that simply loading the data will allow your users to gain business knowledge is an unrealistic view of a data warehouse. Likewise, simply making a front end tool available will not ensure success.
- A DSS application is a 'starter set' of predefined reports created in your front end tool to accommodate the need for different levels of users to have pre-built reports to begin their analysis.

■ Different classes of tools are currently on the market: report writers, data access/query tools, advanced decision support tools, and multidimensional database management systems. These tools can have single or multi-tiered architectures.

■ General data access characteristics are visualization of the data warehouse, formulation of the request, processing the request, and presentation of the results.

■ There are two types of metadata in the world of decision support. The first type of metadata contains information about how your operational systems map into your data warehouse, and may include original system information, field names, and data transformation information. The second type, DSS metadata, is information about how your data warehouse maps to your ends user's front end data access tool.

■ Evolutionary or architectural changes to the data warehouse can be reflected in your DSS application by using DSS metadata as the intermediate link.

■ In large scale deployments, shared metadata can significantly reduce maintenance costs when the metadata is used as the link between the client application and the data warehouse. When the structure of the warehouse is altered, the shared metadata can be changed centrally and the client applications will be updated automatically and transparently.

Chapter 9

Training, Support, and Rollout

SUCCESS CRITERIA

How will you know that your data warehouse and decision support system is successful? If you do not set measurement criteria, you may never know. Some candidate measures include:

- Increased CPU utilization.
- Number of workstations installed.
- Number of users trained.
- Number of logons per day.
- Total logon time/average logon time.
- Improved business: revenue, share, sales, profit.
- Better business decisions being made.

Any of the above could be valid for your organization. The hard part is to develop a method to track progress. Some information can be tracked by the system. Other methods will require that end users take the time to note successes when they occur. You need to look at the goals for your decision support system, your corporate culture, and how the company tracks progress in other areas, and define some measurement criteria. These will change over time as your user community changes, the system evolves, and the capabilities of the system are exploited.

TRAINING

I cannot emphasize enough the importance of training for a successful data warehouse implementation. Consider the following:

- Your users are undoubtedly much more comfortable receiving reports, even if they have to go to five different reports for their information, than learning a whole new sophisticated system. The status quo will seem easier.

- Learning to think in a multidimensional, heuristic mode is a skill set that is learned and improved as it is used. It is quite different from a flat file mindset.

- Most users have no idea and cannot visualize the breadth of functionality sophisticated decision support tools offer.

- Front end data access tools are not simple to use. In fact, they can be relatively difficult.

- The data warehouse is not an operational system. In many cases, users don't *have* to use it; they can *choose* to use it to do their jobs. If you want your data warehouse to bring real value to the corporation, it has to be used.

The most successful data warehouse implementations create ongoing, well-designed and implemented training programs for their user communities. Training should be focused on:

- An introduction to data warehouse concepts.

- An introduction to your own data, where it is in the warehouse, and how it relates to reports or systems the user already knows.

- The mechanics of using the tool. It is important for people to understand basic navigation within the tool.

- The type of analysis that can be performed.

- Using the tool against your own data. What starter set of reports has been developed, how to use them, and how they are organized.

The optimal learning environment may be a customized class created either internally or by a vendor, using a subset of your own data. This approach has the following advantages:

- Uses data that users know and can identify with.

- Provides custom training material and manuals.

■ Provides formal exercises and materials to assist in training new personnel.

It is very important to understand that a multiple-day course at a vendor site is not enough training for the average user. These tools are extremely sophisticated. Often users get confused by the overload of information or forget the information before having a chance to use it. It is imperative that procedures and programs be implemented that can provide ongoing assistance and training on the data warehouse and the front-end tool of choice.

SUPPORT

In order to ensure success, you will need to develop a support structure and plan an approach. When people are using the system, the questions will flow. If you are not getting ANY questions, chances are that no one is using the system. The questions will range across the board to include:

■ Questions about the validity of the data itself.
■ How to use the data, what calculations make sense, and what levels of aggregation are valid.
■ How to pick a report.
■ How report measures were calculated.
■ How to use the applications.
■ How to change an application.
■ How to build your own application.

This first and most obvious method of support is to create and expand the help desk. This gives the client one place to call. The people at your help desk need to be skilled enough to work their way through a technical problem, but also need to have an understanding of the business, the data that is in the warehouse, and how it can/should be used. This complete skill set may not reside with one single person, but you can set up a team that can cover the entire spectrum.

INTERNAL MARKETING OF THE DATA WAREHOUSE

Chances are pretty good that you have not have been in the business of marketing the systems you have developed. This is one aspect of building a data warehouse that can be quite different from developing an operational system. You may need to spend time internally selling the data warehouse. The warehouse is a considerable investment for your organization and it is a new way to do business. Any change is not easy, and cultural changes are especially difficult. So what can you do? How do you get people to use the warehouse?

You must develop a strategy to encourage use. But you must keep in mind your goal—to excite interest in using the warehouse while simultaneously managing expectations. Make sure that people understand when their data will be available and what types of analyses they can perform with it. Some ideas on internally marketing your data warehouse follow.

DATA WAREHOUSE MARKETING IDEAS

Target Specific Groups

Identify two groups of people within the end user community: the technically adept and key influencers in the business group. Target these two groups. The first group will have an interest in new technology and will be able to use the front end tool fairly quickly. Early investments with this group will get them off and running. This group can feed success to management and colleagues.

The second group, the influencers, are important because they are the thought leaders; others watch what they do and follow. If you are lucky, these two characteristics may be found in the same group of people. If not, bring the influencers in early, and have them help make decisions—perhaps in the priority of development. Have them on the project team. When you are rolling out to other users, they will then be in a position to explain to others the advantages of the system. Early success with key influencers will cause others to feel that they need to keep up which will make them more willing to invest time in learning. The more they learn, the more they will use the system. The more they use the system, the bigger the benefits and return to the corporation.

Get Clear and Visible Management Support

Other ways to getting people to invest their time and energy in the data warehouse comes with clear and visible management support. This comes in a variety of flavors:

- Include use of DSS/data warehouse in annual performance goals.
- Provide visible management recognition when people use it.
- Have key executives request information from the warehouse or, when provided with information, respond positively. Sometimes a simple e-mail will motivate people to learn more.

Provide Visible Opportunities

Provide visible opportunities for people to share and learn from each other. Set up brown bag lunches or breakfast meetings once a month to display the capabilities of the system to users who are not yet using it.

- Set up a quorum of advanced decision support users, so they can share new analysis and ways to use the data.

Be Proactive

Another key to providing support is to be proactive. A help desk provides the foundation we all expect, but this is only reactive. It works when the user takes the time to try to use the system and then also takes the time to call. Often, many people don't even know where to begin and therefore, never even call for help. To reach this group of people, apply the same principles as management by wandering around. Place one or more people from the support team in the user work area. These people should be aware of general activity and be on hand to provide assistance and tutoring. Actively helping people over their initial fear of the new system and assisting in their learning curve is a proactive and usually successful way to get users to use the data warehouse.

Create a Publication

Start a newsletter, or get a column in an existing newsletter.

PLANNING A ROLLOUT: DEPLOYMENT

Phased Rollout Approach

Consider the ramifications of bringing hundreds of users on-line at the same time. The support load alone should be enough to scare those thoughts away. The most successful approach is to set up a schedule to bring new groups of people on-line every few weeks or so. This way, you can schedule people for training, then when they get back they will have the live application ready to use on their workstations.

You should plan for greater amounts of time between the first few groups. This will allow you to make any adjustments to the application and/or approach before the next group comes into training. After you work the wrinkles out, then you can run several classes a week. You should consider having two introductory classes a week initially. Then move to one intro class and one advanced class each week.

The phased rollout also provides you with the opportunity to track support requirements and add more staff if required.

Logistics of a Rollout

As you get closer to releasing your decision support system for production use, you need to plan how you intend to distribute the software and/or applications to the users. The cleanest implementations occur when the front end software tool is separate from the database application. One of the key requirements for any large scale deployment is the ability to share the fundamental objects of the application. Object sharing allows an organization to efficiently and effectively demand and deliver information without requiring hundreds of users to constantly "reinvent the wheel". Then, central modification of the reports can be immediately shared by all users. If you have elected not to use a metadata-driven approach to your front end data access, you need to develop a strategy for distributing new applications to the users. If you are distributing the application to remote users, you might consider using electronic software distribution tools.

SUMMARY

In this chapter, you should have learned the following:

- Define some success criteria for your data warehouse so that you can track the progress of the data warehouse in your environment.
- User training and support is one of the most important aspects of building a successful data warehouse.

■ Learning to think and work in a multidimensional, heuristic mode is a skill set that is learned and improved over time.

■ The data warehouse is not an operational system—in many cases the users do not HAVE to use it. And if it is too difficult to use or appropriate levels of training and support are not supplied, they probably won't use it.

■ You must be proactive in getting users to use and appreciate your data warehouse.

■ For a successful data warehouse, plan your in-house marketing and support structures as part of your implementation. Several examples of in-house marketing were supplied in this chapter.

Appendix I

Product Listings

Below you will find a partial list of products that may be valuable in your effort to provide business solutions through the development of a data warehouse. The author is not endorsing any particular product but providing this information as a service to the reader. Omissions of certain products were due to logistics and timing, not to any preference on the part of the author. These product descriptions are directly from the vendor, with only minor modifications. If there are other products that you feel should be included on this list, you may send information to WAREHS@aol.com.

DATA ACCESS AND ANALYSIS

Acumate Enterprise Solution (ES)

Acumate ES is a business intelligence system, based on a multidimensional database engine, that allow managers and knowledge workers to transform huge volumes of corporate data into actionable business information. It provides a set of on-line analytical processing (OLAP) tools, in a client/server environment, that combines the analytical power of a decision support system (DSS) with the ease-of-use of an executive information system (EIS).

Product components include: *Multiway*—a robust multidimensional database engine and stored procedural language; *Acutrieve*—an off-the-shelf analyst workbench; *Spreadsheet Add-in*—a plug-in application that allows spreadsheets to front-end large volumes of multidimensional data; and *Acumate VBX's*—a Visual Basic toolkit for developing custom OLAP applications.

Database server features scalable architecture, object-oriented stored procedural language, powerful analysis tools, and multi-user client/server implementation. Client applications feature open APIs, GUI toolkit, off-the-shelf applications for data loading, analysis and reporting, as well as instructional on-screen co-pilots that step users through complex analysis. This product family complements a data warehousing strategy by delivering an end-to-end Data Retailing solution from data extraction, consolidation, and staging to end-user access, analysis, and reporting.

from: **Kenan Technologies**

Andyne GQL

Andyne provided visual access to SQL-compatible database systems in 1989 when it unveiled *Andyne GQL (Graphical Query Language)*—a decision support suite that offers business users easy-to-understand views of their corporate data. GQL—for *Windows, Macintosh,* and *Unix/Motif* desktops—is an application that helps users build a personally tailored information center as they point and click their way through ad hoc queries and reports.

from: **Andyne Computing Limited**

Andyne PaBLO®

Andyne PaBLO is decision support software for multidimensional data sources that lets business people focus on their business as they explore the information in their corporate data warehouses. Running on *Microsoft Windows* and Apple *Macintosh* desktops, *PaBLO* allows users to browse through multiple dimensions of data, dragging and dropping information to gain new perspectives on their business. *PaBLO* reads advanced, multidimensional HyperCube data sources in popular relational database systems, on file servers, and on the desktop. *PaBLO* also accesses existing multidimensional database systems, such as Arbor Software's *Essbase*.

from: **Andyne Computing Limited**

BrioQuery™

BrioQuery™ from Brio Technology, is a complete ad hoc visual query and analysis tool with built in cross-tabs and easy reporting designed especially for data warehouses. It features an optional Data Model Repository for central management of shared queries and Automatic Distributed Refresh (ADR) capabilities.

BrioQuery, available for *Windows* and *Macintosh,* is a query product which focuses on the analysis of data, not just the production of reports. *BrioQuery* places a fast multi-dimensional analysis tool at the heart of an advanced ad hoc SQL query system. This powerful analysis engine supports an intuitive, interactive "DataPivot®-style" interface. *BrioQuery* also includes a graphical query request builder, a flexible, one-step band-style reporter and high-level scripting for building desktop EIS systems. This combination of powerful features in a single, easy-to- use package makes *BrioQuery* a good choice for IS and end users. *BrioQuery* makes the construction of Data Models—complete query environments which provide centralized control, extend security, and enhanced user comprehension—totally optional.

BrioQuery is available in three configurations: Designer, Navigator, and Explorer. Each is pre-configured to access a wide variety of databases. *BrioQuery* includes native support for *Oracle, Sybase, Red Brick Warehouse,* and *Microsoft SQL Server* and provides access to more than 50 other databases via *SequeLink,* EDA/SQL, DAL and ODBC.

from: **Brio Technology, Inc.**

DSS Agent™ 3.0

DSS Agent is a powerful decision support system that provides access to information for analysis, presentation, integration, and action. Advanced functionality such as Intelligent Agents, Data Surfing, OLAP analyses, and Alerts automate white-collar tasks and aid end-users in making critical business decisions. *DSS Agent* is an open systems product which allows organizations to leverage their existing investments in relational databases and hardware infrastructure. Its scalable interface makes *DSS Agent* the appropriate tool for meeting the full spectrum of DSS needs, ranging from ad hoc query analysis to structured DSS to high-level Executive Information Systems (EIS).

from: **MicroStrategy, Inc.**

DSS Architect™ 3.0

DSS Architect is a tool for defining the multidimensional analysis model and metadata link used in MicroStategy's decision support systems. With DSS Architect, decision support applications are configured, not custom coded. This configuration without programming allows for a multidimensional model that leverages data in relational databases without having to store that data in a multidimensional format. *DSS Architect* adds flexibility to a MicroStrategy decision support system by enabling organizations to quickly and easily update and refine their DSS model, thereby eliminating the need for time consuming and expensive code changes. Changes in the data warehouse can be immediately reflected across hundreds of desktops.

from: **MicroStrategy, Inc.**

DSS Server™ 3.0

DSS Server is an advanced OLAP Server that provides decision support systems with a powerful three tier architecture. The OLAP Engine supports advanced On-line Analytical Processing capabilities including complex derived analysis metrics (market share, contribution, penetration, etc.) and advanced comparison analyses (this year vs. last year, comparable stores, etc.), previously only possible via multidimensional databases. Client machines are released for other tasks while DSS analyses are executed on the server, the load on the RDBMS is smoothed, greater system scalability is achieved, and performance metrics are generated for data warehouse optimization.

from: **MicroStrategy, Inc.**

Intelligent Query (IQ)

IQ is a client/server ad hoc query and reporting tool which empowers end users with data access, analysis and reporting capabilities. It balances the ease of use and rich functionality required by the business user. Users don't need to speak SQL or other database jargon. *IQ* produces row/column style queries,

WYSIWYG report formats, mailing labels, crosstab (matrix) reports and multiple chart and graph formats.

from: **IQ Software Corp.**

IQ Access

IQ Access enables end users to selectively retrieve, reformat and transfer corporate data into popular PC desktop applications (such as *Excel* or *Word*). The data can be filtered and sorted, and calculations can be performed while *IQ Access* reformats data into properly formatted .XLS, .WK3, .DBF, .DAT and many other PC application file types.

from: **IQ Software Corp.**

IQ Professional

The first in a family of object-oriented report writing tools, *IQ Professional* combines programming-like functionality with *Windows* ease-of-use. It supports full WYSIWIG report formatting, and data manipulation. In addition, *IQ Professional* can perform "child reports" and direct the output into the current report format. *IQ Professional* supports multiple formats for headings, body areas, and subtotals, and even allows each area format to be conditional.

from: **IQ Software Corp.**

IQ SmartServer

IQ SmartServer provides *Unix-* and NT-server based performance and functionality to the IQ family of desktop tools. *IQ SmartServer* includes the *AccessManager,* (flexible database access), *SmartSentry* (powerful user and group security), *ResourceManager* (background processing), *SmartScheduler* (scheduling and monitoring of IQ queries and reports), and *Personal DataStore* (data subsetting) modules.

from: **IQ Software Corp.**

ProdeaBeacon

ProdeaBeacon is a decision support product that provides on-line analytical processing (OLAP) capabilities, working directly with industry standard relational databases. Based on a three-tier, or "second generation" client/server architecture, *ProdeaBeacon* brings high performance and enterprise scalability to the data warehouse-based business analysis environment. In addition, *ProdeaBeacon* includes ProactiveAgents, which facilitate decision support workflow by automating entire analytical processes.

from: **Prodea**

SAS System

The *SAS System*—an integrated suite of information delivery software for business decision making—provides organizations with tools to access, manage, analyze, and present their data within an applications development environment. The *SAS System* offers a complete data warehouse solution for a broad range of computing environments. The software provides 1) access to various operational data stores; 2) transformation of data from a variety of environments supported by the software before delivery to the decision-support environment; and 3) exploitation tools for business intelligence. Seamlessly integrated, the *SAS System* is also interoperable with components from other vendors.

from: **SAS Institute Inc.**

Software Interfaces *Pro*REPORTS *

A next generation report writer that enables users to design *ad hoc* and production-quality reports on a client and run on a server.

from: **PLATINUM** *technology, inc.*

Software Interfaces SQLASSIST *

A *Windows*-based query and reporting tool for end users who need to access data throughout the enterprise, view/analyze the data, and integrate with such desktop tools as *Excel, Lotus,* SAS datasets, and others.

from: **PLATINUM** *technology, inc.*

Trinzic Forest and Trees *
PC-based tool that allows power users to analyze warehouse data and drill down to increasing levels of detail through a graphical user interface.

from: **PLATINUM** *technology, inc.*

Trinzic InfoBroker *
Allows end users to use three retrieval methods to access operational and warehouse data directly through *Lotus Notes*, providing for the distribution of data based on *Notes* forms.

from: **PLATINUM** *technology, inc.*

DATA CLEANSING AND CONSOLIDATION

Integrity Data Re-engineering Tool™
The *Integrity Data Re-engineering Tool™* is a highly specialized software toolset and methodology for investigating, standardizing and consolidating data from disparate legacy systems. Reconditioned information can then be mapped easily to databases supporting data warehouses, customer information systems and client/server applications. *Integrity* applies lexical analysis, pattern processing and a powerful statistical matching engine to transform a "hodge podge" of operational data into an accurate, consolidated view of customers and the business. *Integrity* attains high data quality from legacy data: without common keys to match on, with multiple, "unaddressable" business entities hidden in text fields; and with data values that stray from their meta-data field descriptions. In addition to fixing data prior to warehouse migrations, *Integrity* is used to validate or enhance a logical data model by uncovering entity types and business rules that the model failed to account for.

from: **Vality Technology**

DATA TRANSFORMATION AND MOVEMENT

DBStar Migration Architect V3

The *DBStar Migration Architect V3,* automates complex aspects of legacy data modeling, re-engineering, migration and data warehouse design including designing new relational databases and redesigning any database. DBStar helps Data Administrators, Systems Analysts, DBAs, and Database Designers create a rational, maintainable, and extendible set of legacy data models and modern relational databases based upon them. It extracts the business rules embedded in legacy data and generates reports on the business rules discovered, resolves data synonyms across multiple data sources, then generates a new normalized logical and physical design that retains all the appropriate business rules of the legacy data.

from: **DBStar, Inc.**

ETI*EXTRACT Tool Suite

The *ETI*EXTRACT Tool Suite* automates and expedites the access, transformation, and movement of high volumes of data in heterogeneous environments, enabling implementation of new technology while preserving investments in legacy systems. By combining extensible data manipulation capabilities with advanced code generation technology and a customized implementation methodology, Evolutionary Technologies' products provide a full set of tools for populating and maintaining data warehouses; migrating to new databases, platforms, and applications; and tying disparate systems together. The Master Toolset supports a powerful metadata facility, providing access to such critical information as schema definitions, source to target mapping, and business rules and/or data transformation logic.

from: **Evolutionary Technologies International**

PLATINUM Fast Load

Quickly loads data to DB2 for MVS tables.

from: **PLATINUM** *technology, inc.*

PLATINUM Fast Unload
Quickly unloads DB2 for MVS data.

from: **PLATINUM** *technology, inc.*

PLATINUM InfoExpress
(formerly *PLATINUM Data Transport*)
Moves large volumes of data from mainframe databases (DB2
for MVS) to client/server databases (DB2 for *OS/2*, DB2 for
AIX, Oracle, Microsoft SQL Server, and *Sybase SQL Server*).

from: **PLATINUM** *technology, inc.*

PLATINUM InfoRefiner (formerly PLATINUM Pipeline)
Moves data from IMS, VSAM, and sequential file structures to
DB2 for MVS; performs data manipulation functions.

from: **PLATINUM** *technology, inc.*

PLATINUM InfoPropagator
An add-on service for *PLATINUM InfoRefiner*; performs refresh
of changed data when updating the warehouse.

from: **PLATINUM** *technology, inc.*

PLATINUM InfoReplicator
A service which is part of *PLATINUM InfoRefiner*; performs a
total refresh each time the warehouse is updated.

from: **PLATINUM** *technology, inc.*

Prism Warehouse Manager
Prism Warehouse Manager provides the foundation for building
and maintaining a data warehouse of consistent, subject-ori-
ented, historical information. It generates code to extract operational data and external data from source databases, integrates
the data from various sources, and then transforms and loads
the integrated data to a choice of target databases on mainframe and client/server platforms. An extensive selection of
built-in transformations allows users to perform the data con-
versions, summarizations, key changes, and structural changes

needed to create a historical perspective of enterprise-wide information.

Prism Warehouse Manager supports a variety of IT and business projects, such as building decision-support systems, implementing client/server architectures, migrating and converting data between different computing platforms, and re-engineering legacy applications and business processes. *Prism Warehouse Manager* runs on a 386 or 486 PC Workstation under *Windows* 3.1x or *OS/2* 2.1. Price ranges from $100,000 to $125,000, depending on configuration.

from: **Prism Solutions, Inc.**

Prism Directory Manager

Prism Directory Manager allows users to build, store and navigate an integrated Information Directory of the meta data, or information about data, in a data warehouse. Similar to the card catalog at a library, *Prism Directory Manager* assists users in finding relevant information for analysis by providing both business and technical views of what data is in the warehouse, where it came from, how it was transformed and how it has changed over time. Customers can also create their own customized views of the meta data to fit their particular requirements.

Prism Directory Manager imports meta data from several sources, including the meta data collected by *Prism Warehouse Manager* during warehouse development, as well as meta data from CASE tools in CDIF format and predefined tab delimited files. It is a client/server application that supports Sybase, Oracle, DB2, Infomix, Teradata and Tandem NonStop SQL as the server database. The client runs on a 486 PC workstation under Windows 3.1 or Window for Workgroup 3.11. Pricing begins at $50,000.

from: **Prism Solutions, Inc.**

Trinzic InfoHub *

Reads mainframe source data (DB2 for MVS, VSAM, IMS, CA-IDMS, and sequential files; in the future also DATA COM and

Model 204) each time the user requests it, then generates SQL-like statements ("faux" SQL) that enable the user to view the data, even non-relational data, as a relational table.

from: **PLATINUM** *technology, inc.*

Trinzic InfoPump *

Performs data refining and moves data between client/server databases (*Oracle, Sybase, SQL Server,* DB2 for *AS/400, Rdb,* DB2 for *OS/2, SQLBase, Netware SQL,* and ASCII files). Can be used in combination with *InfoHub* to support host-based data formats

from: **PLATINUM** *technology, inc.*

DATABASES

Red Brick Warehouse VPT

Red Brick Warehouse VPT is a parallel relational database product that significantly improves functionality and performance, with particular emphasis on organization, availability, and administration for data warehouse applications. It accomplishes this through support for databases up to 500 gigabytes (GBs) and beyond and greater than one billion records, parallel processing on demand, and time-based data management. It debuted in November, 1994, simultaneously on six of the most widely-used *Unix* platforms, and provides a scalable solution to two of the most significant trends confronting IS managers: the need to manage and reconcile growing amounts of data, and the need to acquire and store a greater range and depth of data.

Red Brick Warehouse VPT introduced two new capabilities that fulfill the promise of parallel processing hardware. Red Brick's *Parallel STARjoin* capability is an "intelligent" optimization algorithm that evaluates each query and utilizes a demand-driven architecture to invoke parallelism automatically and only when necessary. Red Brick's *SuperScan* capability uses each I/O as efficiently as possible. *Red Brick Warehouse VPT* lowers the average response time per query, setting a new benchmark for decision support performance.

Pricing begins at $72,000, based on system configuration. *Red Brick Warehouse VPT* is fully compatible with previous versions of *Red Brick Warehouse.*

from: **Red Brick Systems Inc.**

Andyne Computing Limited
552 Princess Street
Kingston, Ontario
Canada K7L 1C7
voice: (613) 548-4355
fax: (613) 548-7801

Brio Technology, Inc.
650 Castro Street, Suite 500
Mountain View, CA 94041
voice: (800) TRY-BRIO
           (415) 961-4110

Evolutionary Technologies International
4301 Westbank Drive, Bldg B
St. 100
Austin, TX 78746
voice: (512) 327-6994

IQ Software Corp.
3295 River Exchange Drive
Suite 550
Norcross, GA 30092
voice: (800) 458-0386
           (404) 446-8880
fax: (404) 448-4088
e-mail: sales@iqsc.com

Kenan Technologies
One Main Street
Cambridge, MA 02142
voice: (617) 225-2200
fax: (617) 225-2220

MicroStrategy, Inc.
8000 Towers Crescent Drive
Vienna, VA
voice: (703) 848-8600
fax: (703) 848-8610
e-mail: info@strategy.com

Prism Solutions, Inc.
480 Oakmead Parkway
Sunnyvale, CA 94086
voice: (408) 481-0240
fax: (408) 481-0260

Prodea
11095 Viking Drive
Suite 225
Eden Prairie, MN 55344-7240
Voice: (612) 942-1000
Fax: (612) 942-1010

Red Brick Systems Inc.
485 Alberto Way
Los Gatos, CA 95032
voice: (408) 399-3200
fax: (408) 399-3277

SAS Institute Inc.
SAS Campus Drive
Cary, NC 27513
Voice: (919) 677-8000
Fax: (919) 677-8123

Vality Technology
286 Congress Street
Boston, MA 02210
voice: (617) 338-0300

Index

A

Ad hoc analysis, 106–107
  parameter based report, 150
Advanced analytics, 163
Advanced decision support tools, 30
Advanced features, 163
Aggregation, 136–137, 157–158
  custom, 157
  nonaggregatable data, 158
  row math, 158
  straight, 157
  strategies, 71
Analytical databases, 4–6
Analytical processing, 3–6, 23
Analytical systems, 3
Application developer, 28
Application development—creating the starter set of
    reports (Phase 7 of DSLC), 75–76, *75*
Architecture, 24–26, *25*, 173
  and infrastructures, 37–62, *52*
  data, 24
  data, for data warehouse, 24
  data warehouse characteristics, 40–45, *41*
"Architecture and infrastructure" pilot, 84
Attributes
  hierarchies, 134–136
  table, 134
Automating data management procedures (Phase 6 of
    DSLC), 74, *75*

B

Basics, 1–19
Batch query processing, 164–165
Business analyses, 107
Business analyst, 28
Business area
  choosing, 89
  warehouses, 45–50, *46*

C

Capacity planning, 71, 73
Case studies/examples
  Community Mutual Insurance Company, 6–13
  CPG Company, 14–17
  data warehouse database design examples, 139–142
  salad dressing example, 131–136
Casual user or novice, 28
Chargebacks, 13
Constraining a request, 158–159
Cross reference/data transformation algorithm, 43
Customer profiles, 87

D

Data
  availability of, 40–45
  definition language (DDL), 31
  modeling, 68–69, 115
  source, 28
  specific information, 107–108
  surfing, 163
  target, 28
Data access, 149
  characteristics, 155–165
  environment, 147–175
  types of, 150–151
Data access/query tools, 29
Database
  designing for data warehouse, 117–145
  design of, 5
  gateway, 34
  read-only, 5, 6, 24, 44
Data design requirements, 169
Data Interpretation System (DIS), 14
Data mapping and transformation (Phase 4 of DSLC),
    71, 71–72
Data requirements
  gathering, 99–116
Data transformation, 30–31
  tools, 31
Data validation and testing (Phase 8 of DSLC), 76,
    76
Data warehouse, 6, 24
  architecture, 40–45
  development, 81–97
  examples of, 6–13
Decision support databases, 120
Decision support development cycle, 34
Decision support life cycle (DSLC), 61–79
  in an architectural environment, 64–65
  issues affecting, 63–64
  phases of, 65–78
Decision support system (DSS), 3, 23–24
  advanced, 167, *168*
  applications, 30, 149, 154–155, 164
  metadata, 33
  technology, 52
Denormalization, 137–139, 163
Deployment, 186–187
  logistics of rollout, 185
  phased rollout, 184–185
Developing the data model, 114–115
Development skills, 94–95
Dimensional business model, 33, 68, 86, 112, *113*,
    114
Dimension tables, 33, 121
Drill(ing) down, 134, 135

E

Entity relationship diagram (ERD), 9, 116
Enterprise data model, 39, 45, *46*
Environment for data access, 24
Exception reporting, 163
Executive information systems (EIS), 30, 167

F

Fact tables, 33, 121, 125–127, *126*
Finance, 86
Front-end software, 84

G

Gateway products, 54, 84
Gathering data requirements, 99–116
    user interviews, 101–112
Gathering data requirements and modeling (Phase 2
    of DSLC), 67–69, *69*
Generic data warehouse architecture, 45–50, 51, *51*
Gigabyte (GB), 34
Goals, clarifying, 90–95
    be sure technical infrastructures are in place, 91
    choose front-end software based on user needs, 95
    clarify team responsibility and final deliverable,
        91–92
    get correct resources, 93–95
    get correct training, 93
    understand architecture, 91
    understand difference between operational and de-
        cision support data, 92–93
Granularity, 33–34
Graphical user interface (GUI), 58
Graphs, 162

H

Health insurance data warehouse database design ex-
    ample, 142, 143
Help desk, 183
Hierarchies, 33, *113*
    attribute, 134–136
    multiple, *135*

I

Implementation, 173
Incentives, 16
Infrastructures, 9, 15–16
    technical, 26, 27
Integrated database, *49*
Internal marketing, 184

Investment data warehouse database design example,
    139, *141*, 142

J

Joint Application Development (JAD) sessions, 8–9

K

Key terms, 19–36

L

LAN, 9, 15, 54
LAN/WAN, 67, 77
Logical data model, 67, 77, 114–115

M

Maps, 163
Marketing, 87
Marketing tools, 182–184
    be proactive, 184
    create publication, 18
    get clear and visible management support, 185
    provide visible opportunities, 183
    target specific group, 182–183
Market segmentation, 87
Megabyte (MB), 34, 56
Metadata, 31–33, 169–171
    application deployment, 171
    navigational tools, 54
    operational vs. DSS, 169–170, *170*
    warehouse changes, 170–171
Metrics and calculated metrics, 156–159
    advanced dimensional, 156
    aggregation, 157–158
    calculated, 156
    simple, 156
    time comparison analysis, 157
    transformation, 156–157
Middleware tools, 31, *32*
MPP platform, 9
Multidimensional database management systems
    (MDBMS), 30, 159, 166, *167*

N

Nonaggregatable data, 158

O

Operational processing, 3–6, 23
Outboard tables, 127, *128*

P

Partitioning, 137
  strategies, 71
Physical database design and development (Phase 3
  of DSLC), 69–71, *70*
Pilot project, 83–87
  as a base, 85–87
  as development project, 85
  purpose and goal, 83–85
Planning (Phase 1 of DSLC), 65–67, *67*
Populating the data warehouse (Phase 5 of DSLC),
  72–73, *74*
Power users, 28
Predecessor systems, 7–8
Price, 173
Processing
  analytical, 3–6, 23
  operational, 3–6, 23
"Proof of concept" pilot, 83

R

Ranking columns, 163
Relational database management system (RDBMS),
  30, 159
Relational database technology, 53
Reports, 159–162
  columnar format, 159
  crosstab format, 159
Report writers, 30, 166, *166*
Request for proposal (RFP), 172–173
Reservation system data warehouse database design
  example, 139, *140*
Rolling up, 134, 135
Rollout (Phase 10 of DSLC), 77–78, *78*

S

Sales analysis, 87
SAS reporting, 9
Scalability, 173
Security, 72
Snapshot, 4
Source data, 28
Sponsor support, 7
SQL training, 9–10
Star database (*see also* Star schema)
  design, 15, 120–122
  structure, 14
Star schema, 33, 70, *114*
  benefits of, 121
  facts and dimensions, 121–122

how to read diagrams, 122–123
  varieties, 122–131
Star schema varieties, 122–131
  multiple fact tables, 125–127
  multi-star, 129–131, *130*
  outboard tables, 127, *128*
  simple, 124–125, *124, 125*
  snowflake schema, *129*
  variations, 127
Subject area warehouses, *48*
Success criteria, 181
Successful data access, 147–175
Support, 173, 183–184
System development life cycle (SDLC), 63

T

Target data, 28
Technical infrastructures, 26, 27, 50, 64
Terabyte (TB), 34, 63
Tools, classes of, 29–30, 165–168
  advanced decision support, 30, 167, *168*
  data access/query, 29, 165, *165*
  executive information systems (EIS), 30, 167
  multidimensional database management systems
    (MDBMS), 30, 166, *167*
  report writers, 30, 166, *166*
  tiered architectures, 167–168
Tools, selecting, 172–175
  key considerations, 173
  request for proposal (RFP), 172–173
Training (Phase 9 of DSLC), 77, *77*
Training, support, and rollout, 177–188
Transaction-processing databases, 119
  characteristics, 119
Transformation tool
  choice, purchase, installation, 55
  vendor training, 55

U

Update/refresh cycle, 72, 84
User interviews, 101–112
  documenting what you heard, 110–111
  purpose, 101–102
  setting up successful, 102, 103
  what to ask, 105–106, 109–110
  what you have to know for DSS, 111–112
  what you create, 106–108
  what you receive, 106
  who to interview, 102–105
  wish list, 108

Users, levels of, 28–29, 151–153, *153*
    application developer, 28–29, 153
    business analyst, 28, 152
    executive, 152
    novice or casual, 28, 152
    power, 28, 152

V

Visualization of data warehouse, 155

About the Authors

Vidette Poe (WAREHS@aol.com) is the President of Strategic Business Solutions, Inc., a consulting company specializing in the design, development, and implementation of the data warehouse. She provides consulting services to assist clients in setting up data warehouse architectures, creating project plans, and moving through the full life cycle development of decision support systems. Vidette also provides on-site training courses on building a data warehouse. Although she now focuses exclusively on decision support systems, Vidette's expertise in data architecture methodologies and relational database design and development developed over nine years of consulting. She can be contacted at Strategic Business Solutions, Inc., 6750 France Avenue, Suite 149, Edina, MN 55435 612-924-9994.

Laura L. Reeves (ReevesLL@aol.com) is the central region Consulting Manager for MicroStrategy, Inc., a leading supplier of advanced decision support software. She previously held a similar position at Metaphor, Inc. Her experience includes the implementation and cost benefit analysis of decision support systems across sales, marketing, merchandising, advertising, market research, pricing, and finance business functions. Over the past 10 years, Laura has architected over 200 data warehouse and decision support systems for more than 100 companies in a wide variety of industries.

Micro Strategy, Inc., is headquartered in Vienna, Virginia, 703-848-8600.

Author's Note

There seems to be some debate about the advantages and disadvantages of relational versus multidimensional technology for building a data warehouse. This book's focus is on building a data warehouse using a relational database because, at the time of writing, that is where I could draw on the most experience to provide fundamental information to the reader. Although multidimensional technology is mentioned only briefly in this book, this is not an indication of any technology preference.

There are certain aspects of building a data warehouse, primarily related to cleansing, consolidating, and updating data on a predefined basis, that are not covered in detail in this book. This was due to time constraints while writing.